The **5**
Minute
PRAYER
PLAN
FOR TEEN GIRLS

Published by Barbour Books, an imprint of Barbour Publishing, Inc., 1810 Barbour Drive, Uhrichsville, Ohio 44683, www.barbourbooks.com

Our mission is to inspire the world with the life-changing message of the Bible.

Member of the
Evangelical Christian
Publishers Association

Printed in the United States of America.

The 5 Minute
PRAYER PLAN
FOR TEEN GIRLS

A Guide to More Focused Prayer

MariLee Parrish

BARBOUR BOOKS
An Imprint of Barbour Publishing, Inc.

Introduction

If you've picked up this book and opened its pages, you likely desire a more powerful and effective prayer life. Have you felt stuck in a repetitive routine of prayer, praying for the same things, people, and situations, in the same manner—sometimes even with the same words?

This practical and inspirational book will open up new ways into prayer with ninety-three "5-Minute" themed plans for daily quiet time. Prayer plans will focus on varied aspects of life such as: beauty, money, purity, freedom, worry, worship, leadership, protection, healing, work, relationships, church, and hope. A handy subject index in the back of the book will help you find these topics quickly.

Each entry includes:

- Minute 1: A scripture to meditate on

- Minutes 2–3: Specific prayer points and questions to consider as you enter a time of prayer

- Minutes 4–5: A jump-starter prayer to springboard you into a time of conversation with God

The prayers in this book have been written with you in mind, each word penned in prayer, asking God to give insight into the needs of those who will pick this book up and begin a new or renewed journey with Him. Deep, heartfelt prayer happens in those quiet moments when you stand transparently before the One with arms wide open to embrace you in unconditional love and allow Him to speak directly to you.

Christ—No More, No Less!

*This mystery has been kept in the dark for a long time,
but now it's out in the open. God wanted everyone, not
just Jews, to know this rich and glorious secret inside
and out, regardless of their background, regardless of
their religious standing. The mystery in a nutshell is just
this: Christ is in you, so therefore you can look forward
to sharing in God's glory. It's that simple. That is the
substance of our Message. We preach Christ, warning
people not to add to the Message. We teach in a spirit
of profound common sense so that we can bring
each person to maturity. To be mature is
to be basic. Christ! No more, no less.*

Colossians 1:26–28 msg

- God wants everyone—including teenage
  girls—to know that Jesus Christ can live in
  you! The same power that raised Jesus from
  the grave is what God offers all of us who believe. Will you accept His gift? Go to God in
  prayer and talk to Him about this. He paid the
  ultimate price to offer you a relationship with
  God. Why? Because He loves you so very
  much! All you have to do is believe and invite
  Him to be your Lord (the boss of your life)
  and Savior (understanding that He paid the
  price for your sins, guaranteeing you eternal
  life with God).

- When you choose to follow Jesus, His very own Spirit comes to live inside you (Romans 8:9)! How amazing is that? He loves you so much that He could never leave you alone down here. Thank Him for the gift of His Spirit inside you. Ask Him to help you understand what that means.

- God wants you to know His voice (Isaiah 30:21; John 10:27). Ask Him to open your ears and your heart so that you can begin hearing Him speak to you.

....

Thank You for coming for me, Jesus. I invite You into my life. I accept that You've paid the price for my sins and that there's nothing I can do to earn Your love or salvation. You've made a way for me to be with God forever. Help me live my life for You. Be the boss of my life. I know You're the loving, encouraging kind—not a demanding taskmaster. Open my ears and my heart so that I can begin hearing from You.

Advice for the Young

*Run from anything that stimulates youthful lusts.
Instead, pursue righteous living, faithfulness, love,
and peace. Enjoy the companionship of those who
call on the Lord with pure hearts. Again I say, don't get
involved in foolish, ignorant arguments that only start
fights. A servant of the Lord must not quarrel but must
be kind to everyone, be able to teach, and be patient
with difficult people. Gently instruct those who oppose
the truth. Perhaps God will change those people's
hearts, and they will learn the truth.*

2 TIMOTHY 2:22–25 NLT

- Paul wrote some letters to Timothy, a young minister, to encourage him not to give up. Paul gave some good advice that God wants us to know still today. Prayerfully read over these verses. Ask God what He wants to teach you through them.

- First Timothy 4:12 (NIV) says: "Don't let anyone look down on you because you are young, but set an example for the believers in speech, in conduct, in love, in faith and in purity." If you've invited Jesus into your life, the Spirit of God is alive in you! The same Spirit lives in each one of us—from children who've recently accepted Christ to believers who've walked with Christ for a lifetime. Christ in you makes all the difference no matter how old you are. He gives you the power to be an example to others, even older generations. You, as a teenager, can inspire and encourage young and old alike. Ask God for help in setting a good example for all people around you.

- Ask God for help to run away from tempting situations and silly disagreements. Ask Him to fill your life with friends and family who love God and are committed to following His ways.

- Ask the Holy Spirit to help you remember this verse: "Greater is he that is in you, than he that is in the world" (1 John 4:4 KJV). With God's power alive and at work in you, you have nothing to be afraid of. Give thanks to God that He is with you always.

....

Thanks for giving me wisdom, Lord, and caring about the fact that I'm young. Thank You that Your Spirit is alive in me, helping me live a pure life out of love for You and those around me.

The Breakthrough

Now to him who is able to do immeasurably more than all we ask or imagine, according to his power that is at work within us, to him be glory in the church and in Christ Jesus throughout all generations, for ever and ever! Amen.

Ephesians 3:20–21 niv

- God is able to do way more than you think He can. Take some time to thank Him for His unlimited greatness.

- Thankfulness can open our hearts to hear from God. Thank Him for the ways that He has shown Himself to you in the past.

- In what ways have you put limits on God? Have you limited the way He is "permitted" to speak to you? Consider the ways that you are comfortable hearing from God: through His Word, through a pastor, through music. What other ways are you able to hear from God? Through nature? For more inspiration, read Psalm 95:1–7, Psalm 96:11–13, and Psalm 19:1–4.

- Our heavenly Father respects our boundaries. If you've put boundaries, limits, and walls between you and God and what He is "allowed" to do in your life, your prayer life could be suffering. Ask God to break down and break through any walls that you have built that might be creating a feeling of distance between you and God.

- Ask God to show Himself to you in new ways. Be open to the work of the Holy Spirit in your heart.

....

God, I am so thankful that You are able to do far beyond anything I could ever imagine. I accept and believe that You can do anything. Open my heart and mind to hear from You in new ways. You created my imagination, and I ask You to use it in whatever way might bring You honor and glory in my life. I don't want to put limits on You, Lord. Break down any walls that I've created that might prevent me from hearing from You. You are the Creator of all things, and I hope to hear You speak to me more through Your creation. Help me see Your everyday miracles all around me and accept them as gifts and messages from You. I want to hear from You, Jesus. I want Your Holy Spirit to be evident in my life. Teach me how to hear from You more and more each day.

From of Old and Forever

Blessed are you, GOD of Israel, our father from of old and forever. To you, O GOD, belong the greatness and the might, the glory, the victory, the majesty, the splendor; yes! Everything in heaven, everything on earth; the kingdom all yours! You've raised yourself high over all. Riches and glory come from you, you're ruler over all; you hold strength and power in the palm of your hand to build up and strengthen all. And here we are, O God, our God, giving thanks to you, praising your splendid Name.

1 CHRONICLES 29:10–13 MSG

- God's Word tells us that He is the same yesterday, today, and forever (Hebrews 13:8). That means that God's miracles you've heard about from the Bible are still possible today. Do you believe that? What might be preventing you from believing in God's power today? Ask God to show you.

- Spend some time in worship. Praise God for who He is and what He's done. Colossians 1:15 tells us that Jesus is the image of the invisible God. Picture Jesus in your mind's eye—in your imagination. Belt out your favorite worship song and picture Jesus receiving your praise.

- Riches and glory and every good gift come from God. Do you have a roof over your head and food on your table? Thank God for that. That means you are wealthier than most of the world's population.

- God holds strength and power in His hands. Are you in need of strength at this time in your life? What are you facing that could use an extra dose of God's power? Ask Him to build you up and strengthen you in His power.

....

Lord, You are the God of the Old Testament and the God of the New. You were powerful then and You're powerful now. I trust that any miracles You've done in the past You are still capable of today. And when I have trouble believing this, please help my unbelief! I worship You today because of who You are: my Creator and the Lover of my soul—the God of all. Every good thing I have is because of You. I'm truly thankful for the ways I've seen Your hand and provision in my life. I believe that true strength and power come from You alone. Would You strengthen my heart today?

Every Chance in the World

That was the last thing the young man expected to hear. And so, crestfallen, he walked away. He was holding on tight to a lot of things, and he couldn't bear to let go. As he watched him go, Jesus told his disciples, "Do you have any idea how difficult it is for the rich to enter God's kingdom? Let me tell you, it's easier to gallop a camel through a needle's eye than for the rich to enter God's kingdom." The disciples were staggered. "Then who has any chance at all?" Jesus looked hard at them and said, "No chance at all if you think you can pull it off yourself. Every chance in the world if you trust God to do it."

MATTHEW 19:22–26 MSG

- A rich man was asking Jesus about eternal life. Jesus told him to go sell everything he owned, give the money to the poor, and follow Him. That's not exactly what the rich man wanted to hear. In fact, it was probably the last thing he wanted to hear! Is Jesus asking you to do anything that seems really difficult? Talk about it with Him now. What is He telling you?

- Jesus wants to talk with each of us individually. What Jesus wants one person to do is not necessarily the same exact thing He wants you to do. Jesus is all about relationship. He is a very personal God. He wants to be your friend and your trusted counselor. He wants you to come to Him first for advice. What do you need advice about today? Ask Jesus for help and guidance. Talk to Him like you would your best friend. You can talk to Him out loud, or you can pray in your heart and mind. It's also very helpful to write down your prayers so you can have a reminder of how God answers!

- As you pray, remind yourself that "with God, all things are possible." That is a truth to memorize and live your life by. Thank God for this truth.

....

God, I believe I have every chance in the world to do whatever it is You want me to do if You are with me. And I don't have to work hard to figure it out. I can rest and trust in You, knowing that You'll lead me where I need to be right when I need to be there.

A Life of Purpose

*For God did not give us a spirit of timidity or
cowardice or fear, but [He has given us a spirit] of
power and of love and of sound judgment and personal
discipline [abilities that result in a calm, well-balanced
mind and self-control]. . .for He delivered us and saved
us and called us with a holy calling [a calling that
leads to a consecrated life—a life set apart—a life of
purpose], not because of our works [or because of any
personal merit—we could do nothing to earn this],
but because of His own purpose and grace
[His amazing, undeserved favor] which was
granted to us in Christ Jesus before the
world began [eternal ages ago].*

2 TIMOTHY 1:7, 9 AMP

- Think of a current situation that you are
  struggling with—one that is totally outside
  your comfort zone. Bring that situation to
  Jesus in prayer.

- You're probably feeling uncomfortable just
  praying about this situation. Notice your
  anxiety and nervousness as you bring the
  problem to mind. Does it cause your heart
  to pound? Do you feel stress in your head
  or neck? Picture Jesus standing in front of
  you. What does He want you to know? Ask
  Jesus to exchange your fears and anxieties

for His power and peace.

- Jesus saves us and delivers us from our fears
  so that we can live a life of purpose. Ask
  Jesus to make His purpose for you clear.
  What are your gifts and talents? What stirs
  your heart in life-giving ways? Pray and listen
  as God writes this purpose on your heart.
  Make sure you write down any answer God
  is giving you. He will always confirm His truth
  for you if you ask Him (Jeremiah 29:13; Jeremiah 33:3; Romans 12:2; James 1:5).

. . . .

*Jesus, I'm so thankful that You want to replace my
fears and anxieties with Your power and purpose. I
ask for You to calm me down. Please fill me with peace
in Your presence. I want to hear from You about my
purpose. I want to live a life set apart for You. It's
amazing to me that You planned for me before the
world even began. I'm Yours, Lord. Use me to bring
Your love and light to others.*

The Armor of God

In conclusion, be strong in the Lord [draw your strength from Him and be empowered through your union with Him] and in the power of His [boundless] might. Put on the full armor of God [for His precepts are like the splendid armor of a heavily-armed soldier], so that you may be able to [successfully] stand up against all the schemes and the strategies and the deceits of the devil.

<small>EPHESIANS 6:10-11 AMP</small>

- As you pray today, open your Bible to Ephesians 6. Read through verses 10–20. Ask the Holy Spirit to bring these scriptures alive for you. Picture yourself putting on the armor of God. Are you tired of defending and protecting yourself? You don't have to! Instead, ask Jesus to cover you with His spiritual armor.

- The belt of truth was also known as the "girdle of truth," or you could call it the "Spanx of truth." The truth keeps everything in the right place. When you are firmly grounded in truth from God's Word, you can stand strong. Ask God to give you a longing and love for His Word.

- The breastplate of righteousness covers your heart. Our righteousness comes from Christ alone (1 Corinthians 1:30). Ask Jesus to wrap His arms around you and protect your heart.

- The shoes of peace can help you walk in His ways (John 14:27). Ask God to help you promote peace in your relationships and have courage to share with others how they can find peace with God.

- The shield of faith protects you from enemy arrows. Ask God to protect you from evil, to guard you from distraction, and to hide you in Christ (Colossians 3:3).

- The helmet of salvation protects your head and your mind. Ask God to give you an eternal perspective as you cover your head daily with the truth of your salvation. Ask Him to protect your mind and keep it pure.

- Finally, the sword of the Spirit is your weapon for defense and offense. It's God's Word (2 Timothy 3:16–17). You need truth from God's Word to effectively defeat the enemy. This is how Jesus defeated the enemy in Matthew 4:1–11. Ask God to help you understand His words so you can use them effectively against your enemy.

....

Thank You, Lord, for giving me Your armor of protection. Please show me how to use this equipment effectively.

No Excuses

For ever since the creation of the world His invisible attributes, His eternal power and divine nature, have been clearly seen, being understood through His workmanship [all His creation, the wonderful things that He has made], so that they [who fail to believe and trust in Him] are without excuse and without defense.

ROMANS 1:20 AMP

- Sometimes it can be hard to believe in a God you can't see. But the Bible tells us that if we take a look at creation all around us and see the amazing things He's made (including you and all other humans!), we are without excuse when it comes to knowing that God is real. Think about five friends or family members that don't believe in God. Bring them to mind and pray for them. Pray that God would open up their eyes to see Him in creation.

- Pray for each of the friends and family members you are focusing on using this prayer: *Father, I pray over _____ today. I pray that they would see the evidence of You all around them today. I ask that Your Holy Spirit would invade their heart in a supernatural way. Remove their heart of stone (Ezekiel 11:19) and give them a heart that makes room for Jesus and His loving ways. Show me how to love them with Your love so they can see that You are alive in me.*

- As you think of these loved ones throughout your day, pray for their hearts to soften. Remember that God loves them even more than you do! People see Jesus through our love, not our arguments and advice about how they should live. Ask Jesus to help you love them with His kind of supernatural love.

....

Lord, my heart is heavy for people I love that don't want You in their lives. I know I can't be the Holy Spirit to them or try to make them live the way I choose to. I bring them before Your throne, God. I ask that You would be real to them in ways they didn't think possible. Help me love them well instead of trying to force my beliefs on them. Let them know love. Let them feel loved. You are love. You are the very source of love. Help them connect that to You.

The Helper

*He told them, "You don't get to know the time.
Timing is the Father's business. What you'll get
is the Holy Spirit. And when the Holy Spirit comes
on you, you will be able to be my witnesses
in Jerusalem, all over Judea and Samaria,
even to the ends of the world."*

Acts 1:7–8 msg

- Praying can be overwhelming at times. But did you know that God gave you a Helper who even helps you pray? Romans 8:26 (esv) tells us: "Likewise the Spirit helps us in our weakness. For we do not know what to pray for as we ought, but the Spirit himself intercedes for us with groanings too deep for words." When you are feeling stuck as you pray, you can simply lift your heart to God and let the Holy Spirit help you.

- Jesus gave us a lot of help with prayer too. Open your Bible to Matthew 6:9–13. Look it up in several translations and then rewrite this prayer in your own words.

- John 14:26 (esv) says: "But the Helper, the Holy Spirit, whom the Father will send in my name, he will teach you all things and bring to your remembrance all that I have said to you." Take some time in prayer to thank God for sending you the Holy Spirit. He is our Counselor, Teacher, Comforter, Convicter, and Guide. The Spirit of God is alive in you. How amazing! Worship God in prayer that He is three in one, the triune God—Father, Son, and Holy Spirit.

- "Come, Holy Spirit" is a simple and powerful prayer. Pray this when you're not sure how or what to pray. When you do this, you're praying in faith that you believe in God's power to keep His promises. He has sent the Holy Spirit to help and to guide. Trust that He will do that.

....

Jesus, thank You for sending me the Holy Spirit as my Helper and Guide. You've given me every single thing I need to live my life for You. Lord, You've thought of everything! When I don't know what to do, I can ask! When I don't know what to pray, You help! Come, Holy Spirit. Fill my heart with the presence of God. Lead me and guide me as I walk this path with You.

Silence

God is our refuge and strength, an ever-present help in trouble. Therefore we will not fear, though the earth give way and the mountains fall into the heart of the sea. . . . Come and see what the LORD has done, the desolations he has brought on the earth. He makes wars cease to the ends of the earth. He breaks the bow and shatters the spear; he burns the shields with fire. He says, "Be still, and know that I am God; I will be exalted among the nations, I will be exalted in the earth." The LORD Almighty is with us; the God of Jacob is our fortress.

PSALM 46:1–2, 8–11 NIV

- Praying to our Father is not about sending off our wish list to heaven and moving on with our day. It's about relationship with our God. He wants to spend time with us as a friend. He wants to comfort and advise us like a wise and loving parent. He wants us to know how much we are loved. Sometimes sitting in the quiet with God is the best way to pray. Ask Him to fill you with His love as you sit quietly in His presence. Picture yourself climbing into God's lap and letting Him parent you. What does He want to show you?

- A refuge is a place of safety and protection. Can you picture yourself being protected by

God? The Bible is full of imagery that we can take to heart. You can imagine the mountains crumbling and falling into the sea, right? How terrifying that would be, standing close by. But God promises that you don't have to be afraid. He is with you. Picture God calming all your fears. Be still before Him in prayer.

- Exodus 14:14 (ESV) says: "The LORD will fight for you, and you have only to be silent." Are there any fears or worries on your mind today? Trust that God is bigger and more powerful than anything you are facing. Tell God that you trust Him.

....

Father God, I bring my whole heart to You today. I rest in You alone. You are the perfect parent, and I trust Your wisdom. You are my refuge and the safest place that I can be. Please fill me with Your love and truth as I sit quietly in Your presence.

The Happy Recipe

I've learned by now to be quite content whatever my circumstances. I'm just as happy with little as with much, with much as with little. I've found the recipe for being happy whether full or hungry, hands full or hands empty. Whatever I have, wherever I am, I can make it through anything in the One who makes me who I am.

PHILIPPIANS 4:11–13 MSG

- Get out your prayer journal and check out Philippians 4:6–7 in the Amplified version: "Do not be anxious or worried about anything, but in everything [every circumstance and situation] by prayer and petition with thanksgiving, continue to make your [specific] requests known to God. And the peace of God [that peace which reassures the heart, that peace] which transcends all understanding, [that peace which] stands guard over your hearts and your minds in Christ Jesus [is yours]." Write this out like you would copy down a recipe with all the ingredients listed in these verses and we'll use it as our prayer guide today.

- God tells us that instead of worrying, we should pray! As you thank and worship God, tell Him what's on your heart. When you do that, God's peace will wash over you.

- Do you feel content, or are you always wishing for the next thing? Ask God to give you contentment today, regardless of your circumstances. You can make it through anything with the Spirit of the living God at work inside you. If you're having trouble feeling God's supernatural peace, this mindset could be the key. As a young person, your whole world can seem like a bubble of friends and school and social media. But God's view of your life is so much more! Ask God to fill you with contentment and thankfulness even if you're struggling with hard times. This doesn't mean you ignore your feelings or pretend that everything's okay when it's not. It's just bringing all those thoughts and feelings to the only One who can help and asking Him to give you an eternal view of your life and circumstances.

....

Lord, I confess I've got some worries that feel pretty big. I struggle with being content in my current situation. I know You can help. I know You see me. I want to believe that I can get through this with You. I ask that You help me see the bigger picture.

Straight from God

God, the one and only—I'll wait as long as he says.
Everything I hope for comes from him, so why not?
He's solid rock under my feet, breathing room for
my soul, an impregnable castle: I'm set for life.
My help and glory are in God—granite-strength and
safe-harbor-God—so trust him absolutely, people;
lay your lives on the line for him. God is a safe place
to be. . . . God said this once and for all;
how many times have I heard it repeated?
"Strength comes straight from God."

Psalm 62:5-8, 11 MSG

- Have you been working hard at something lately? Maybe school or sports? Are you trying to make yourself stronger in those areas? There is nothing wrong with that! The important thing to remember is that strength comes from God Himself. He can help! Bring to mind everything you are currently working hard on. Ask for His supernatural power. He has all the answers and is very interested in helping you! Maybe it's algebra, maybe it's gymnastics, maybe it's basketball or trigonometry. . .ask God to help you think clearly. Ask for His strength.

- How are you at giving glory to God when you achieve good results? When you crush that test or score that goal? Ask God to help you get in the habit of thanking Him when you achieve your goals. Memorize this truth and pray it out loud: "I can do everything through Christ, who gives me strength" (Philippians 4:13 NLT).

- As His Word promises, God is a safe place to be, and you can trust Him absolutely. Thank Him for being a safe refuge for you. When you mess up and when you succeed, God is safe. He delights in you. He shares your sorrows and your joys. Allow Him to be with you in those times. Bring your successes and failures to Jesus now, and let Him love you in them.

....

Lord God, You are the solid Rock under my feet. I believe it's true that everything I hope for comes from You. You have the answers I'm looking for. You are the source of strength that I'm needing. I bring You my successes and my failures. I don't have to perform for You. You love me no matter what. I believe that nothing can separate me from Your love!

The Power of God
Directed toward You

He is not weak or ineffective in dealing with you,
but powerful within you. For even though He was
crucified in weakness [yielding Himself], yet He lives
[resurrected] by the power of God [His Father]. For we
too are weak in Him [as He was humanly weak], yet we
are alive and well [in fellowship] with Him because
of the power of God directed toward you.

2 CORINTHIANS 13:3–4 AMP

- God loves you so much that He gave His
  only Son for you (John 3:16). Jesus is all the
  fullness of God (Colossians 2:9), and He is
  the image of the invisible God (Colossians
  1:15). Jesus is God in human flesh. He chose to
  yield Himself and give His life for you. Sit in
  God's presence now and ask Him to give you
  a greater understanding of what this means.
  Accept His great love for you and praise Him
  for His power directed toward you.

- Ask Jesus to answer these questions for you:
  Is He mad at you? Is He disappointed in you?
  Wait in silence. Focus your thoughts on Jesus
  as you wait expectantly for His loving reply.
  Psalm 5:3 (NIV) says: "In the morning, LORD,
  you hear my voice; in the morning I lay my

requests before you and wait expectantly." Do as the psalmist did.

- God's Word tells us that God is powerful within us and that we are in fellowship with Him because of God's power directed toward us. We can have a deep and meaningful prayer life because of this truth. Again, prayer is not wishful thinking. It's about relationship. Talk to God now in your heart or out loud and wait for His response. He wants to be your loving parent and best friend. Sometimes He will point you to a scripture. Sometimes He will put a picture in your imagination. He might put a worship song in your mind. He may impress your heart with a strong idea or thought. The ways that our Creator can speak to us are unlimited.

....

God, I believe in Your unlimited power directed toward me. I want to hear from You in any way You want to speak. I invite You to invade all parts of my life. Help me see You and hear from You.

The Truth about Who You Are in Christ

For the word of God is living and active and full of power [making it operative, energizing, and effective]. It is sharper than any two-edged sword, penetrating as far as the division of the soul and spirit [the completeness of a person], and of both joints and marrow [the deepest parts of our nature], exposing and judging the very thoughts and intentions of the heart.

HEBREWS 4:12 AMP

Knowing who you are in Christ will change your whole life forever. Bring these scriptures before Jesus, and ask Him to help you accept each of them as truth.

- I am free and clean in the blood of Christ (Galatians 5:1; 1 John 1:7).

- It is no longer I who live, but Christ who lives in me (Galatians 2:20).

- He has rescued me from darkness and has brought me into His kingdom (Colossians 1:13).

- I am a precious child of the Father (Isaiah 43:6-7; John 1:12; Galatians 3:26).

- God sings over me (Zephaniah 3:17).

- He delights in me (Psalm 149:4).

- I am a friend of Christ (John 15:15).

- Nothing can separate me from God's love (Romans 8:38–39).

- God knows me intimately (Psalm 139).

- God sees me as beautiful, and I am wonderfully made (Psalm 139:14; Ecclesiastes 3:11).

- God is for me, not against me (Romans 8:31).

Make Psalm 139:1–10 (NLT) your prayer for today:

. . . .

"O LORD, you have examined my heart and know everything about me. You know when I sit down or stand up. You know my thoughts even when I'm far away. You see me when I travel and when I rest at home. You know everything I do. You know what I am going to say even before I say it, LORD. You go before me and follow me. You place your hand of blessing on my head. Such knowledge is too wonderful for me, too great for me to understand! I can never escape from your Spirit! I can never get away from your presence! If I go up to heaven, you are there; if I go down to the grave, you are there. If I ride the wings of the morning, if I dwell by the farthest oceans, even there your hand will guide me, and your strength will support me." I believe everything You say about me, God! Thank You for Your love.

When God Helps

*I pray to you, O LORD, my rock. Do not turn a deaf ear
to me. For if you are silent, I might as well give up and
die. Listen to my prayer for mercy as I cry out to you
for help, as I lift my hands toward your holy sanctuary.
. . . The LORD is my strength and shield. I trust him
with all my heart. He helps me, and my heart is filled
with joy. I burst out in songs of thanksgiving. The LORD
gives his people strength. He is a safe fortress for his
anointed king. Save your people! Bless Israel,
your special possession. Lead them like a shepherd,
and carry them in your arms forever.*

PSALM 28:1-2, 7-9 NLT

- You can be totally honest with God. You can't
  hide anything from Him anyway. He already
  knows how you feel about everything. Is
  there any thought or feeling that you are
  stuffing down and not able to fully admit
  even to yourself? Ask Jesus to bring it to the
  surface.

- The psalms are full of sometimes brutal
  honesty. God is the safest place for you to
  share everything. He can shine His light on
  all your thoughts and feelings and help you
  work them out. Ask God to bring anything to
  light that needs to be discussed and worked
  through.

- When God helps, He turns darkness and stress and sadness into joy and singing and thanksgiving! It's always a process. God values you, and He is careful with you. He leads you like a gentle shepherd carries his sheep. When you allow Him to help you work through your issues and feelings, miraculous things happen. He knows exactly what you need and how to get you from one step to the next. Say yes to God's help as you pray.

- Picture yourself being carried in the arms of Jesus. What does Jesus want you to know? What truth does He want you to remember forever?

....

God, I am so thankful that You are a safe place. In fact, You are my safest place. Help me long for You and desire to be with You every day. Help me create a special time and place for me to rest in Your arms as You speak love and truth over me. Help me listen. Cast away my fears. I want to be totally honest with You.

The Name above All Names

And [so that you will begin to know] what the immeasurable and unlimited and surpassing greatness of His [active, spiritual] power is in us who believe. These are in accordance with the working of His mighty strength which He produced in Christ when He raised Him from the dead and seated Him at His own right hand in the heavenly places, far above all rule and authority and power and dominion [whether angelic or human], and [far above] every name that is named [above every title that can be conferred], not only in this age and world but also in the one to come.

EPHESIANS 1:19–21 AMP

- The name of Jesus is powerful. Some of the most powerful prayers are simply "Jesus!" In those moments you are declaring His power and asking for His help and protection. Philippians 2:10 (NLT) tells us that "at the name of Jesus every knee should bow, in heaven and on earth and under the earth." Are you afraid? Are you in need of Jesus to come and rescue? Say His name!

- Ask Jesus if there is an area in your life or a certain situation where He wants to increase your faith in Him. What is He showing you?

- Jeremiah 33:3 (NIV) says: "Call to me and I will answer you and tell you great and unsearchable things you do not know." Ask Jesus to come through for you in whatever way you need right now. Ask Him to be real to you. Ask Him to hold your hand. Rest in His goodness and His great love for you.

- The power of God is unlimited! Ask God to write this truth on your heart. If you are struggling with doubt, bring that to Jesus too. Ask Him if there are any lies you are believing that could be preventing you from accepting the truth of His limitless power in your life.

....

Jesus, I believe You are all-powerful. You are beyond my understanding and fully capable of taking care of everything I need. I ask that You erase any lies the enemy has been writing on my heart and fill me with Your truth. I want to trust You more. Continue to be real to me. Cultivate our relationship in a way that affects my everyday life.

Jesus Himself

Going through a long line of prophets, God has been addressing our ancestors in different ways for centuries. Recently he spoke to us directly through his Son. By his Son, God created the world in the beginning, and it will all belong to the Son at the end. This Son perfectly mirrors God, and is stamped with God's nature. He holds everything together by what he says—powerful words!

Hebrews 1:1–3 msg

- Through Jesus Himself, God created and saved the world. Jesus is God in the flesh. When you look at Jesus, you get a clear picture of God. And He can speak directly to you. You may not hear an audible voice, but Jesus can speak to your heart just the same. And He will make Himself clear to you if you seek Him. Ask Jesus to speak clearly to you today. What is He impressing on your heart?

- When you hear from Jesus, it will line up with His Word. If you are not sure whether something is from your imagination or from God, simply ask. Ask Jesus to confirm what you've heard. If it is from God, you'll find that it lines up with scripture, and even if the message is challenging or convicting, the end result will bring life and love. You may receive confirmation from another believer, from a song, from a message at church, or any number of ways that God wants to make His voice clear to you. Are you listening for Him to speak?

- Getting to know the voice of God is one of life's greatest adventures. When Jesus confirms that He's spoken to you, pay attention to what that sounds like and feels like. Sometimes it's a gut check when something around you seems off or wrong. Sometimes it's a sweet whisper of love and acceptance in a cool breeze. Listen for God to answer when you pray.

....

Jesus, I long to know Your voice. Help me recognize You as You speak to me. Help me pay attention when You are talking to me so that I am able to discern Your voice better and better as I grow up. Show me that it's really You. I know that if I ignore Your voice, I'll eventually stop hearing from You altogether. Help me follow Your promptings and heart checks as they come.

Closer Than You Think

*I sought the LORD, and he answered me; he delivered
me from all my fears. Those who look to him are
radiant; their faces are never covered with shame.
This poor man called, and the LORD heard him;
he saved him out of all his troubles. The angel of the
LORD encamps around those who fear him, and he
delivers them. Taste and see that the LORD is good;
blessed is the one who takes refuge in him. . . .
The eyes of the LORD are on the righteous, and his ears
are attentive to their cry; but the face of the LORD is
against those who do evil, to blot out their name from
the earth. The righteous cry out, and the LORD hears
them; he delivers them from all their troubles.
The LORD is close to the brokenhearted and
saves those who are crushed in spirit.*

PSALM 34:4–8, 15–18 NIV

- Jesus is closer than you think sometimes.
When your heart is broken, Jesus is with you.
When your spirit feels crushed, God is close.
Bring to Jesus any sadness that is heavy on
your heart right now. Ask Him to be with you.

- God's Word says that He hears your prayers
and His eyes are on you. He sees you. You
are important to God, and He loves you more
than you could ever imagine. Sit in God's
presence and let Him love you.

- Are you having a hard time feeling God's presence or His love? Pray and ask God if there is a lie you are believing that is preventing you from believing in God's love for you.

- Sometimes Christians can be great at telling others about the love of Jesus but have a lot of trouble believing it for themselves. Read the following verse and speak it out loud as you pray: "See what great love the Father has lavished on us, that we should be called children of God! And that is what we are!" (1 John 3:1 NIV).

....

Father, I confess I struggle with believing that You could love me so much! Forgive me for not trusting that I'm important to You. Show me anything that is preventing me from having a deep and loving relationship with You. Help me accept the truth that I'm Your child and You love me like no other!

Raw Power

*But the LORD is the true God and the God who is
Truth; He is the living God and the everlasting King.
The earth quakes and shudders at His wrath, and the
nations are not able to endure His indignation. . . . God
made the earth by His power; He established the world
by His wisdom and by His understanding and skill He
has stretched out the heavens. When He utters His
voice, there is a tumult of waters in the heavens,
and He causes the clouds and the mist to ascend
from the end of the earth; He makes lightning
for the rain, and brings out the wind from His
treasuries and from His storehouses.*

JEREMIAH 10:10, 12–13 AMP

- The God who loves and cares about you is
  the same God who stretched out the heavens. How amazing is that? It might be hard to
  believe, but the Bible tells us it's true. As you
  go to Him in prayer, thank Him for His raw
  power and unfailing love.

- When you think about God's unlimited power
  and love for you, what happens to your
  problems? Do you trust that God can handle
  anything you've got going on? Talk to Him
  about the problems on your mind. Ask Him
  to help!

- If God speaks water into existence at the sound of His voice, He can take care of anything you are facing. Praise Him for His awesome power. Cast all your cares on Him in prayer; He cares for you (1 Peter 5:7)!

- Our God is the God of truth and the only true God. We might try to put things in God's place to make us feel better about ourselves, and those things become idols. They take attention off God in our lives. Maybe it's people or sports or fashion or social media. Open your heart to God and ask Him to reveal anything that you have made into an idol. Confess it and allow God to take His rightful place in your life.

....

I'm amazed at Your power, Lord God. You made the mountains and the oceans, and yet You care deeply for me. I don't understand it all, but I'm truly thankful. I bring You my cares and my frustrations. I know You want to help. Please remove the idols I've created to try to take care of things on my own. You have my heart, Lord.

The Singing God

Sing, O daughter of Zion; shout aloud, O Israel!
Be glad and rejoice with all your heart, O daughter
of Jerusalem! For the LORD will remove his hand of
judgment and will disperse the armies of your enemy.
And the LORD himself, the King of Israel, will live
among you! At last your troubles will be over, and
you will never again fear disaster. On that day the
announcement to Jerusalem will be, "Cheer up, Zion!
Don't be afraid! For the LORD your God is living among
you. He is a mighty savior. He will take delight in you
with gladness. With his love, he will calm all your
fears. He will rejoice over you with joyful songs."

ZEPHANIAH 3:14–17 NLT

- Getting to know God through reading His Word and prayer will change your life. God renews our minds as we come to Him in this way. He transforms us and makes us more like His Son. Pray and ask God to begin transforming and renewing your mind.

- Rewrite Romans 12:1–2 (NIV) as a prayer in your own words: "Therefore, I urge you, brothers and sisters, in view of God's mercy, to offer your bodies as a living sacrifice, holy and pleasing to God—this is your true and proper worship. Do not conform to the pattern of this world, but be transformed by the renewing of your mind. Then you will be able to test and approve what God's will is—his good, pleasing and perfect will."

- As you get to know God, you will find that He's so much more than you ever thought possible. He is all-knowing, all-powerful, the Savior of the world, and yet the Bible tells us that He sings over us! Thank Him in prayer for knowing you so intimately.

- God delights in you. He is proud of you. He sees you through the lens of Jesus. Nothing can make Him love you more or less. You cannot work for God's love. It just is. Let that truth sink in as you come before Him in prayer.

....

Lord, I want to know Your will. I want to know Your words and Your truth for my life. Transform me as I offer my life to You as a living sacrifice. I accept Your astonishing love for me. I praise You and thank You for caring about me and showing me Your ways.

Bring Your Plans to Jesus

*Trust in and rely confidently on the LORD with all
your heart and do not rely on your own insight or
understanding. In all your ways know and acknowledge
and recognize Him, and He will make your
paths straight and smooth [removing
obstacles that block your way].*

PROVERBS 3:5–6 AMP

- Decision-making is not as difficult as we make it. As a young person, you have tons of decisions to make in your life. But God cares about them all. Think about all the decisions on your mind right now and bring them to Jesus.

- When we forget that God wants to help us make choices, we get confused and anxious. When we leave God out of the decision-making process, it causes lots of unnecessary problems. Confess this to God in prayer. Ask forgiveness for the times you've left God out of the equation. Repent and ask God to help transform your thinking in this area.

- Do you trust that God cares for you? Do you trust that He is all-powerful and has good plans for you? Do you believe He wants to help you make decisions? Tell Him.

- Now, bring your current decisions back to your mind. Picture yourself inviting Jesus into each choice you need to make. Ask for help and direction. The Bible says that He wants to make your paths straight and smooth. He will remove the obstacles that block your way to His will when you ask Him. Do this in prayer.

- Are you planning a party or a vacation with friends? Ask God to be a part of it. Are you planning your high school classes or picking out colleges? Invite Jesus in. Let Him be your guide. Pull out your calendar as you pray today. Ask Jesus to be a part of every single thing you have going on.

....

Lord, I trust that You care about everything I have on my schedule. I invite You to be a part of every plan and every decision. Remind me that You're here when I start to forget You. Forgive me for the times I've done this. You're my best friend, and I want You to be involved in everything I do. Help me be willing to change course if I feel You leading me in a different way. Give me ears to hear.

Powerful Truth

We faithfully preach the truth. God's power is working in us. We use the weapons of righteousness in the right hand for attack and the left hand for defense. We serve God whether people honor us or despise us, whether they slander us or praise us. We are honest, but they call us impostors. We are ignored, even though we are well known. We live close to death, but we are still alive. We have been beaten, but we have not been killed. Our hearts ache, but we always have joy. We are poor, but we give spiritual riches to others. We own nothing, and yet we have everything.

2 CORINTHIANS 6:7–10 NLT

- Do you find yourself trying too hard to fit in? Do you worry about what others are saying and thinking about you? When God's power is at work in you, you can be confident in who you are as His child no matter what anyone else thinks. Come to Jesus in prayer and tell Him what you're worried about. Have people you thought were friends gossiped about you? Share it with Jesus. He wants to comfort you and carry your burdens.

- Rumors and lies can definitely hurt. But as you bring them to Jesus, He reminds you of the truth. You are a dearly loved daughter of the King of kings! You have access to all of God's riches and knowledge. You can go boldly before the throne of God because of how loved you are. What truth do you need to be reminded of today? Go to God in prayer and ask Him to speak the truth you need to hear.

- Being confident in who you are in Christ comes from spending time with God in His Word and in prayer. This God-confidence allows you to keep your chin up when things around you seem overwhelming. Like today's scripture says, even if your heart aches, you can still have joy. Ask God to fill you with His joy and confidence.

....

Thank You for the powerful work You are doing in my heart, Lord. Forgive me for trying so hard to fit in when You've called me to be myself. And who I am in You is what matters most. Fill me with Your supernatural joy when the sadness of things happening around me seems overwhelming.

No One Like You

*O Lord, you are so good, so ready to forgive, so full
of unfailing love for all who ask for your help. Listen
closely to my prayer, O Lord; hear my urgent cry. I will
call to you whenever I'm in trouble, and you will answer
me. No pagan god is like you, O Lord. None can do
what you do! All the nations you made will come and
bow before you, Lord; they will praise your holy name.
For you are great and perform wonderful deeds. You
alone are God. Teach me your ways, O Lord, that I
may live according to your truth! Grant me purity of
heart, so that I may honor you. With all my heart I will
praise you, O Lord my God. I will give glory to your
name forever, for your love for me is very great. You
have rescued me from the depths of death.*

PSALM 86:5–13 NLT

- The time you spend with God will accomplish
more than anything else you could ever do.
There is no one else who can do what God
can do. Come before Him in prayer and thank
Him for His unfailing love and concern for
you.

- Jeremiah 32:17 (ESV) says: "Ah, Lord GOD!
It is you who have made the heavens and
the earth by your great power and by your
outstretched arm! Nothing is too hard for
you." Speak this truth to God as your prayer.

Ask Him to help you believe that He can do anything and can change anyone's mind or plans. Is there a problem on your mind right now that you need help with? Ask for God to intervene. Nothing is too hard for Him.

- Ask God to teach you His ways so that you can follow His will for your life. Ask Him to purify your heart and your mind so that you can think His thoughts. Ask Him to help you plan your day so that you can spend quality time with Him in prayer.

....

God of All, there is no one like You. I am so blessed to be able to bring everything on my heart to You in prayer—and to know that You want to help! That never ceases to amaze me. I praise You with all my heart, Lord. You have rescued me and loved me like no other.

Being Transformed

Therefore, since we have such a hope, we are very bold. We are not like Moses, who would put a veil over his face to prevent the Israelites from seeing the end of what was passing away. But their minds were made dull, for to this day the same veil remains when the old covenant is read. It has not been removed, because only in Christ is it taken away. Even to this day when Moses is read, a veil covers their hearts. But whenever anyone turns to the Lord, the veil is taken away. Now the Lord is the Spirit, and where the Spirit of the Lord is, there is freedom. And we all, who with unveiled faces contemplate the Lord's glory, are being transformed into his image with ever-increasing glory, which comes from the Lord, who is the Spirit.

2 Corinthians 3:12–18 NIV

- When Moses met with God, it transformed everything about him. Even his skin was glowing with the radiance of God's glory—so much so that Moses wore a veil so that others wouldn't be afraid to come near him. Without Jesus, a veil covers our hearts from being able to see and hear from God. As you turn to God in prayer, ask Him to remove the veil and anything else that might prevent you from experiencing God.

- When you experience God face-to-face,

He transforms you into His image. You are being transformed in many ways already, as you grow up. You're changing from being a child and transforming little by little into the woman that God designed you to be. Invite God into this transformation. Allow Him access to every part of you. Tell Him that you want Him to re-create and renew your every thought and action.

- Growing up and transforming can be difficult. A caterpillar has to stop eating, hang upside down, and spin itself into a cocoon where the metamorphosis occurs before it can become a butterfly. When you come face-to-face with God, there is freedom and love and help for your transformation process. Ask God to be with you as He prepares you to fly.

....

God, thank You for making a way for me to have a face-to-face relationship with You through Jesus. I fully submit to this transformation process that You designed for me.

Face-to-Face

*Now Moses used to take a tent and pitch it outside
the camp some distance away, calling it the "tent of
meeting." Anyone inquiring of the LORD would go to
the tent of meeting outside the camp. And whenever
Moses went out to the tent, all the people rose and
stood at the entrances to their tents, watching Moses
until he entered the tent. As Moses went into the tent,
the pillar of cloud would come down and stay at the
entrance, while the LORD spoke with Moses. Whenever
the people saw the pillar of cloud standing at the
entrance to the tent, they all stood and worshiped,
each at the entrance to their tent. The LORD
would speak to Moses face to face,
as one speaks to a friend.*

EXODUS 33:7–11 NIV

- In Old Testament times, a face-to-face
  relationship with God wasn't possible for
  most people. Jesus hadn't come to earth yet.
  Moses was favored and chosen by God to
  lead, so God spent special, face-to-face time
  with Moses while the others looked on. Now,
  because of all that Jesus has done for us on
  the cross, He made a way for all of us to have
  a special, face-to-face relationship with God.
  Thank God in prayer for sending Jesus to
  make a way for us to know God.

- God spoke to Moses just like a friend. John 15:15 (NIV) says: "I no longer call you servants, because a servant does not know his master's business. Instead, I have called you friends, for everything that I learned from my Father I have made known to you." Jesus calls us His friends now. As you pray, talk to God just like you would your friends. Do you write your friends texts and notes? Write a note to God as your prayer today.

- A face-to-face friendship with God is not something to take for granted. Remember, it wasn't even possible for most people back in Moses' time. Now, God has chosen you to be His friend. What feelings does this stir up in your heart? Talk to God about them.

....

God, I'm honored and amazed that You call me Your friend. Thank You for making a way through Jesus for us to be friends. This is so huge! Help me never take it for granted.

He Knows Your Name

*Moses said to the LORD, "You have been telling me,
'Lead these people,' but you have not let me know
whom you will send with me. You have said, 'I know you
by name and you have found favor with me.' If you are
pleased with me, teach me your ways so I may know
you and continue to find favor with you. Remember
that this nation is your people." The LORD replied,
"My Presence will go with you, and I will give you rest."
Then Moses said to him, "If your Presence does
not go with us, do not send us up from here.
How will anyone know that you are pleased with
me and with your people unless you go with us?
What else will distinguish me and your people from
all the other people on the face of the earth?"
And the LORD said to Moses, "I will do the very
thing you have asked, because I am pleased
with you and I know you by name."*

EXODUS 33:12-17 NIV

- No matter where you are or what kind of
  personality you have, God is calling you to be
  a leader. If you tend to be quiet and shy, God
  can use you to lead with a gentle strength
  in many situations. If you are outgoing and
  extroverted, God can use your spirit of
  enthusiasm to share His love with many. The
  point is to allow God to use the personality

that He's given you in the way that He wants to. In prayer, offer your personality up to God. Thank Him for giving you exactly what He wanted you to have. Ask Him to lead you as you lead others.

- God knows your name and everything about you. He set you on earth at this exact time in history for a purpose. He wants you to know Him. He wants you to love Him and love others through Him. Ask for His presence to go with you wherever you go. Ask Him to lead you and to teach you His ways.

- Sit in the presence of God and just be you. Tell God how much you love Him. Enjoy being fully known and fully loved.

....

It's still hard to believe that You know everything about me and love me anyway, Lord. But Your Word tells me it's true. Lead me as I grow up and lead the people around me.

You Can Trust Him

*He didn't tiptoe around God's promise asking
cautiously skeptical questions. He plunged into
the promise and came up strong, ready for God,
sure that God would make good on what he had said.
That's why it is said, "Abraham was declared fit before
God by trusting God to set him right." But it's not
just Abraham; it's also us! The same thing gets
said about us when we embrace and believe the
One who brought Jesus to life when the conditions
were equally hopeless. The sacrificed Jesus
made us fit for God, set us right with God.*

ROMANS 4:20–25 MSG

- Are you or a close friend or family member
  facing a situation that seems a bit hopeless?
  Talk to Jesus about it. Tell Him all the details.

- As you share the details of the situation with
  God in prayer, ask Him to remind you of His
  goodness and faithfulness. Ask Him to remind
  you of His power. Ask Him to help.

- When you are staring at a large, steep mountain knowing that you have to reach the top
  to resolve an issue, things can look pretty
  scary and hopeless. But what if you get closer
  to the mountain and see that a small, smooth
  path circles around the mountain, all the way

to the top? You'll find that you were worried and stressed for nothing! Are you facing a mountain of problems? Bring your anxiety and fears to Jesus and ask Him to make your path smooth.

- Use Isaiah 26:3 (NIV) as a prayer: *Lord, Your Word says, "You will keep in perfect peace those whose minds are steadfast, because they trust in you." I ask for that peace to fill me as I trust You. Help me focus on You and Your faithfulness.*

....

Father, just like Abraham, I want to trust You whole-heartedly! I know You're gonna make good on all Your promises to me. Remove all my doubts and skepticism. I confess my lack of faith and focus in times when I'm just too busy. I'm learning that You are bigger than any mountain I face and that sometimes things aren't always as they seem. Help me look for You and Your way in every situation I face.

Whispers of Power

*"God stretches the northern sky over empty space
and hangs the earth on nothing. He wraps the rain in
his thick clouds, and the clouds don't burst with the
weight. He covers the face of the moon, shrouding
it with his clouds. He created the horizon when he
separated the waters; he set the boundary between
day and night. The foundations of heaven tremble;
they shudder at his rebuke. By his power the sea grew
calm. By his skill he crushed the great sea monster."
His Spirit made the heavens beautiful, and his
power pierced the gliding serpent. These are just
the beginning of all that he does, merely a
whisper of his power. Who, then, can
comprehend the thunder of his power?"*

JOB 26:7-14 NLT

- Reflect on these verses from Job. Replace
  each reference to God with *You* and make
  this your prayer to Him. For example: *"You
  stretch the sky over empty space and hang
  the earth on nothing. You wrap the rain in
  Your thick clouds. . ."*

- Think about the great power of God. Imagine
  Him creating the world and hanging the earth
  on nothing! Worship Him in prayer.

- Verse 14 tells us that this is just the beginning,

a mere whisper of His great power! And this all-powerful God has His thoughts set on you. He loves you more than you could ever understand. Ask Him to help you hear His whispers. Be listening for His still, small voice.

- Isaiah 41:10 (ESV) says: "Fear not, for I am with you; be not dismayed, for I am your God; I will strengthen you, I will help you, I will uphold you with my righteous right hand." Agree with this scripture in prayer. Confess your fears to God and ask for His strength and help.

....

God, I love to read these scriptures of Your awesome power. And to think, all You've done is just a glimpse of what You're capable of! It's beyond my human understanding. But I'm so grateful that You think of me. I believe You know me and that You love me more than anyone else ever could. I bring my fears to You and trust that You are beyond capable of taking care of everything. Give me ears to hear Your whispers. I want to know for sure that I'm hearing Your voice.

Ask, Seek, Knock

*"So I say to you: Ask and it will be given to you; seek
and you will find; knock and the door will be opened
to you. For everyone who asks receives; the one who
seeks finds; and to the one who knocks, the door will
be opened. Which of you fathers, if your son asks for a
fish, will give him a snake instead? Or if he asks for an
egg, will give him a scorpion? If you then, though you
are evil, know how to give good gifts to your children,
how much more will your Father in heaven give
the Holy Spirit to those who ask him!"*

LUKE 11:9–13 NIV

- God wants you to ask, seek, and knock. Let's
  start with ask. God wants us to come to Him
  in prayer and ask Him anything. James 4:2
  (NIV) says: "You do not have because you do
  not ask God." A lot of times we forget to
  bring things to God first. We try to get our
  needs met through other people and other
  things, when God is just waiting for us to
  come to Him. What do you need to talk to
  Him about today? What can you ask Him that
  you haven't yet?

- Seek. Jeremiah 29:13 (NIV) says: "You will seek
  me and find me when you seek me with all
  your heart." What does seeking God with all

your heart mean? Bring this verse to God in prayer. Ask Him to show you what it means to seek Him with all your heart. He is close; He is not far away. . .and He wants to be found! Remember, He's not playing games with you. You can know Him well—like family. Like a best friend.

- Knock. Luke tells us we can knock on God's door and be invited in, but did you know that Jesus is knocking on your door too? Revelation 3:20 tells us this truth. Jesus is always knocking at the door of your heart. Will you let Him in? Talk to Him about it.

. . . .

Jesus, thank You that You want to be found by me! Show me how to get into a rhythm of coming to You about everything. You've knocked on my heart, and I'm letting You in. I trust that You are a good Dad. The perfect parent. You know exactly what I need, and You always give the perfect gifts. I love You, Lord.

The Blessings of God

"God blesses those who are poor and realize their need for him, for the Kingdom of Heaven is theirs. God blesses those who mourn, for they will be comforted. God blesses those who are humble, for they will inherit the whole earth. God blesses those who hunger and thirst for justice, for they will be satisfied. God blesses those who are merciful, for they will be shown mercy. God blesses those whose hearts are pure, for they will see God. God blesses those who work for peace, for they will be called the children of God. God blesses those who are persecuted for doing right, for the Kingdom of Heaven is theirs."

MATTHEW 5:3–10 NLT

- Asking for God's blessing is something we see throughout the entire Bible. Jesus blessed people. People blessed God. And leaders often blessed their followers. Asking for God's blessing is asking for His purpose and power in your life, not asking Him to give you everything you want. What do you need God to bless? Ask Him for His blessing in this area.

- Psalm 103:1–2 (AMP) says: "Bless and affectionately praise the LORD, O my soul, and all that is [deep] within me, bless His holy name. Bless and affectionately praise the

LORD, O my soul, and do not forget any of His benefits." Think about how you could bless God. Then do it!

- Read 1 Chronicles 4:10. Jabez asked God for a big blessing. Can you write a similar prayer to God?

- Matthew 5:3–12 is known as the Beatitudes. They show how to be blessed in God's kingdom. As you read through the Beatitudes, are there any areas where you need God to show up and help? Do you struggle with purity or being humble? Ask for God's blessing. Ask for His supernatural power to help you in your struggle.

....

I'm asking for Your blessing on my life, Lord. I need to see Your purpose and power in my world. Bless my calling, and show me what path You would have me take that is honoring to You. Bless my family and be real to them. Help me love them with Your love inside of me. And I bless You too, Lord. I praise You for who You are and what You are doing in my heart.

The Door Is Open

Peter fairly exploded with his good news: "It's God's own truth, nothing could be plainer: God plays no favorites! It makes no difference who you are or where you're from—if you want God and are ready to do as he says, the door is open. The Message he sent to the children of Israel—that through Jesus Christ everything is being put together again—well, he's doing it everywhere, among everyone. You know the story of what happened in Judea. It began in Galilee after John preached a total life-change. Then Jesus arrived from Nazareth, anointed by God with the Holy Spirit, ready for action. He went through the country helping people and healing everyone who was beaten down by the Devil. He was able to do all this because God was with him."

ACTS 10:34–38 MSG

- The Bible says that God doesn't play favorites (Galatians 3:28). We are all equal because of Jesus. He loves each of us as if there was only one of us to love! The love of Jesus is for everyone! God's door is wide open. Are you aware of any situation where favorites are being played? Pray for God's justice to prevail.

- Do you have any friends that have been victims of racism or bullying? Do you have any friends that have been left out because of the way they look? Ask for God to comfort those friends. Pray for them to find peace and love. Ask God what you might be able to do to help.

- God is with you, and He can help you stand up to injustice when He calls you to. If you know someone who is being hurt by someone else and doesn't have the strength to get help, God calls us to get involved. Proverbs 31:8 (NIV) tells us to "speak up for those who cannot speak for themselves, for the rights of all who are destitute."

....

Thank You, Lord, that Your door is open to everyone! You love each of us abundantly and equally. Thank You for seeing me and my friends. You know and You care. I pray for protection over the ones that are not being treated fairly. Would You please show me if I am supposed to help in some way? I ask for wisdom. Would You make the way clear to me? Thank You that this matters to You!

The Source of Hope

Because of our faith, Christ has brought us into this place of undeserved privilege where we now stand, and we confidently and joyfully look forward to sharing God's glory. We can rejoice, too, when we run into problems and trials, for we know that they help us develop endurance. And endurance develops strength of character, and character strengthens our confident hope of salvation. And this hope will not lead to disappointment. For we know how dearly God loves us, because he has given us the Holy Spirit to fill our hearts with his love.

ROMANS 5:2–5 NLT

- The Holy Spirit fills our hearts with the love of God. And that same power is what gives us hope. Read Romans 15:13 (NLT): "I pray that God, the source of hope, will fill you completely with joy and peace because you trust in him. Then you will overflow with confident hope through the power of the Holy Spirit." Make this verse your own personal prayer today: *God, Source of Hope, please fill me completely with joy and peace because I trust You. Please fill me with confident hope through the power of the Holy Spirit.*

- Think of some disappointments you've faced in your lifetime. Have you greatly hoped for something and then it never happened? Bring those memories to Jesus and allow Him to comfort you.

- Our hope of heaven is one that will never disappoint us. And not only that, we can have great hope in Christ during this lifetime. Because of Jesus, we can have a vibrant and powerful relationship with God right now. We don't have to wait for heaven to know Him and experience His peace. He always keeps His promises. He will be faithful to you. He is always there. He sees you, and He's working everything out for your good (Romans 8:28). Take some time in prayer and thank God for the hope He's already given you. Thank Him for His faithfulness.

....

Jesus, thank You for giving me a living hope. Because of You, I can have a real-life relationship with God. I bring my disappointments to You and ask that You would comfort me as we sort them out together. Thank You for showing Yourself to me and working everything out for my good. I know You will never let me down. Fill me with Your supernatural peace.

You Are with Me

Even though I walk through the [sunless] valley of the shadow of death, I fear no evil, for You are with me; Your rod [to protect] and Your staff [to guide], they comfort and console me. You prepare a table before me in the presence of my enemies. You have anointed and refreshed my head with oil; my cup overflows. Surely goodness and mercy and unfailing love shall follow me all the days of my life, and I shall dwell forever [throughout all my days] in the house and in the presence of the LORD.

PSALM 23:4–6 AMP

- God has promised to be with us through everything. Check out Matthew 28:20 (MSG): "I'll be with you as you do this, day after day after day, right up to the end of the age." Jesus promises that He'll be with us "day after day after day." Thank Him in prayer that He is with you right now.

- Psalm 23 reminds us that we don't have to wait for heaven to start living in the kingdom of God. Jesus came to give us abundant life here and now and for all eternity. Take a moment to think about what you believe concerning eternal life. Bring these thoughts to Jesus in prayer. Is there anything that you have believed about the kingdom of God that isn't true? Ask Jesus to make that clear to you.

- God is with us in the good times and the bad. Are there any dark valleys you are going through right now? Ask Jesus to walk with you through them. Ask Him for a sense of His presence and His peace. What does He want you to know as you are going through hard times? Ask Him.

- We have the promise of God's goodness, His mercy, and His unfailing love. . .right now and for all eternity! Praise Him for those promises. Do you trust Him to keep those promises? Tell Him!

....

Father, thank You for being with me at all times. Thank You for having my back and walking with me on every path I take. I trust in Your promises. I am confident that You will do what You say You're going to do! I accept the truth that Your goodness, mercy, and unfailing love will cover me all the days of my life. Now and for all eternity.

Fresh Fruit

But the fruit of the Spirit [the result of His presence within us] is love [unselfish concern for others], joy, [inner] peace, patience [not the ability to wait, but how we act while waiting], kindness, goodness, faithfulness, gentleness, self-control. Against such things there is no law. And those who belong to Christ Jesus have crucified the sinful nature together with its passions and appetites. If we [claim to] live by the [Holy] Spirit, we must also walk by the Spirit [with personal integrity, godly character, and moral courage—our conduct empowered by the Holy Spirit].

GALATIANS 5:22–25 AMP

- Who doesn't love fresh fruit? The Bible talks about a different kind of fruit—spiritual fruit. When we invite Jesus to be the Lord of our lives, His presence within us starts changing and transforming us. . .this produces fresh, spiritual fruit. In Matthew 7:20, Jesus tells us that we can recognize people by their fruit. The evidence of fruit in their lives will tell you if they are good or bad. Healthy or unhealthy. Open your heart to God in prayer. Ask Him to show you if you are producing healthy spiritual fruit.

- If God is convicting you about something, it means He loves you and wants you to grow.

Confess anything that needs confessing.

- Pruning is a method of gardening where you cut off dead branches or stems. Through pruning, the plant becomes healthier and can produce more fruit. Ask God to shine a light on any area of your heart that needs pruning.

- Make a list of the fruit of the Spirit in your prayer journal. Ask God to fill you with love, joy, peace, patience, kindness, goodness, faithfulness, gentleness, and self-control. Look up scriptures that have to do with each spiritual fruit. Use those scriptures as prayers, and ask the Holy Spirit to increase these fruits in your life.

....

God, I open up my heart for You to take a good look inside of me. I invite You into every area of my life. Show me where I need more of You. I want to produce fresh, healthy fruit so that others can see that You are at work in me. Prune me where I need pruning. Fill me with the fruit of Your Spirit alive in me.

Gifts and Surprises

*This is my life work: helping people understand and
respond to this Message. It came as a sheer gift to me,
a real surprise, God handling all the details. When it
came to presenting the Message to people who had
no background in God's way, I was the least qualified
of any of the available Christians. God saw to it that I
was equipped, but you can be sure that it had
nothing to do with my natural abilities.*

EPHESIANS 3:7–8 MSG

- When we accept the call of God on our life,
  He blesses us with divine gifts and surprises!
  Paul said that his life's work was to help people understand and respond to the Gospel
  of Jesus Christ. Paul didn't feel qualified or
  equipped, and the fact that God called him to
  do this was a real surprise and a gift to Paul.
  What gifts has God given you? Thank Him for
  making you special.

- Like Paul, do you feel like you've been put
  in a position that is beyond your natural
  abilities? When that happens, the power of
  God shows up big-time! Is God calling you to
  do something that feels out of your comfort
  zone? Ask God to show you if He has something like this for you to do.

- When God stretches you, He always provides the tools you need to succeed. He will show up when you depend on His strength. Where do you need God to show up? Where do you need more of His strength? Take this to Him in prayer. What does He want you to know?

- Where do you need God to handle the details? Are you worrying too much about a situation that you've been placed in? Are you carrying more than you should or trying to make things happen when it's not quite the right time? Confess this to God in prayer. Ask forgiveness for trying to do too much without allowing God to handle the details. Ask for His help in this area.

....

Lord, thank You for the gifts You've given me. I want to use them to show others how much You love them. And I want to use them to show my love for You. I trust that if You've called me into a scary situation that feels beyond what I can do, You will show up. You'll handle the details. You'll provide the power I need to get the job done.

Strength for the Weary

*He gives strength to the weary, and to him who has
no might He increases power. Even youths grow weary
and tired, and vigorous young men stumble badly,
but those who wait for the LORD [who expect, look for,
and hope in Him] will gain new strength and renew
their power; they will lift up their wings [and rise
up close to God] like eagles [rising toward the
sun]; they will run and not become weary,
they will walk and not grow tired.*

ISAIAH 40:29–31 AMP

- Are you in need of strength from God? Most of us could use a strong dose of God's power in our lives on a daily basis. To think clearly as you're learning. To conquer projects and tasks that you need to graduate. To lead in areas where you feel inadequate. The Bible tells us that those of us who wait for the Lord—those of us who pray—will gain new strength! Go to God in prayer now and ask Him for His strength and power.

- Waiting for the Lord in prayer means that you expect Him to show up and keep His promises. You look for Him, and you put your hope in Him. Take these expectations before His throne. Tell Him how you feel.

- As Jesus pours His life into you, you are refilled with living water. John 7:38 (NIV) says: "Whoever believes in me, as Scripture has said, rivers of living water will flow from within them." What does it look like to have rivers of living water flowing from within you? Ask Jesus to show you.

- Think of the areas of your life where you feel inadequate right now. Where do you feel like you are not enough? Where do you feel like you just can't do something? Bring those thoughts and feelings to Jesus. What truth does He want you to know about these feelings?

....

Lord, Your Word tells me that You give strength to the weary and that You give power to those who feel like they have none. . .if we will simply come to You in prayer and wait expectantly. I trust in Your promises. I believe that You are faithful. I believe that You will provide everything I need to live the life You have called me to. In the places where I feel powerless, Lord God, please fill me with Your supernatural power. Pour Your very life into me.

Prayer Transforms Us

*About eight days after Jesus said this, he took
Peter, John and James with him and went up onto a
mountain to pray. As he was praying, the appearance
of his face changed, and his clothes became as bright
as a flash of lightning. Two men, Moses and Elijah,
appeared in glorious splendor, talking with Jesus.
They spoke about his departure, which he was about
to bring to fulfillment at Jerusalem. Peter and his
companions were very sleepy, but when they became
fully awake, they saw his glory and the two men
standing with him. As the men were leaving Jesus,
Peter said to him, "Master, it is good for us to be here."*

LUKE 9:28–33 NIV

- The Bible says that Jesus often went away
  to be alone with God and pray. As believers,
  our power and hope and strength to make it
  through each day come from our time spent
  with God. Like Jesus, our time spent in prayer
  transforms us. Begin your prayer today by
  asking Jesus to meet you where you are and
  to begin transforming you.

- Jesus lived a life of prayer. He was dependent
  on His time with God, and He modeled that
  for us. What does it mean to live a life of
  prayer? Ask God what He wants you to know
  about your time spent with Him.

- When you are living a life of prayer, you don't just say a few words to God, give Him your wish list for the day, then after you say "Amen," shut the door to God until tomorrow. No. You invite Him into every moment of your day. You seek His thoughts when you need help. You ask for Him to give you love for others as you work with people throughout the day. You tell Him you love Him. You thank Him for His presence in your life. Try those things right now as you invite Jesus to be a part of your day.

....

Jesus, I invite You into every moment of my day. Remind me that You are with me at all times. Nudge me by Your Holy Spirit to acknowledge You throughout this day. Let me see You at work in my life. I invite You to begin transforming me. I want to live a life of prayer just like You did. Help me learn Your ways.

Powerful Praise

Praise the LORD! For it is good to sing praises to our [gracious and majestic] God; praise is becoming and appropriate. The LORD is building up Jerusalem; He is gathering [together] the exiles of Israel. He heals the brokenhearted and binds up their wounds [healing their pain and comforting their sorrow]. He counts the number of the stars; He calls them all by their names. Great is our [majestic and mighty] Lord and abundant in strength; His understanding is inexhaustible [infinite, boundless].

PSALM 147:1–5 AMP

- We praise God for who He is and what He is doing. In your times of prayer, have you ever just praised God instead of asking for things? Take some time right now to declare the greatness of God. Worship Him in prayer. Focus on His goodness and greatness alone. Thank Him for who He is. Sing to Him in praise.

- When you begin your prayer in thankfulness, your focus shifts from your problems to the powerful goodness of God. Can He handle your problems? Of course. Is there anything too big or too little for God? No way. What else can you thank Him for in prayer?

- God is in the business of healing broken hearts and comforting people in their pain and sadness. Is someone you know going through an extremely hard time? Lift that person up to Jesus. Ask for God to be real to them in ways they've never experienced. If He knows the number and names of all the stars, He certainly knows and cares about your friend. Ask God if He wants you to share that with your friend in some special way.

- The Bible reminds us over and over that God is far beyond our human understanding. Things are rarely what they seem. Ask God to give you new eyes to begin seeing things from His perspective.

....

God, I worship You and praise You for who You are. You are the Creator and Sustainer of all things. You've given me life, and I'm so thankful that I can know You personally. Thank You for being so real to me. I trust that You can handle everything I've got going on. I lift my hurting friends to You. Show me how to share Your amazing love with them. You know all things, and I ask that You would give me new eyes to see life from an eternal perspective.

Reaping What You've Sown

Remember this: Whoever sows sparingly will also reap sparingly, and whoever sows generously will also reap generously. Each of you should give what you have decided in your heart to give, not reluctantly or under compulsion, for God loves a cheerful giver. And God is able to bless you abundantly, so that in all things at all times, having all that you need, you will abound in every good work. As it is written: "They have freely scattered their gifts to the poor; their righteousness endures forever." Now he who supplies seed to the sower and bread for food will also supply and increase your store of seed and will enlarge the harvest of your righteousness. You will be enriched in every way so that you can be generous on every occasion, and through us your generosity will result in thanksgiving to God.

2 CORINTHIANS 9:6-11 NIV

- Are you familiar with the law of sowing and reaping? It means that what you plant is what you harvest. It's true in the natural world, and it's true in the spiritual world. If you plant pumpkins, you'll harvest pumpkins. If you plant doubt and worry in your heart, that's exactly what will grow. Galatians 6:7 also tells us that a person reaps what they sow. There are rewards for sowing good things and consequences for sowing evil. Have you planted good things or harmful things? Are you sowing the fruit of the Spirit? Bring this to God in prayer. Ask Him to supernaturally uproot any wrong seed that you have planted.

- When you plant generosity in your heart, you reap blessings. Generosity results in thanksgiving. Are you a cheerful giver, or do you have a hard time sharing what you've worked so hard for? Ask God to help you share what He has so generously given you.

- Remember, when Jesus Christ is firmly planted in your heart, the fruit of the Spirit begins to grow. Ask Jesus what it means to be firmly planted in Him. What is He trying to show you?

....

Jesus, again I ask You to look through my heart and find anything that is out of line with You. Dig up any seed that should not be growing roots in my life. Pluck out the weeds and help me sow good seed instead. I want Your fruit to be evident in my life.

Staying Close to the Shepherd

The LORD is my Shepherd [to feed, to guide and to shield me], I shall not want. He lets me lie down in green pastures; He leads me beside the still and quiet waters. He refreshes and restores my soul (life); He leads me in the paths of righteousness for His name's sake.

PSALM 23:1–3 AMP

- In Bible times, shepherds were part of everyday life. References to shepherds are made throughout much of the Bible. Jesus tells us many times that He is our Shepherd. Read the following verses and prayerfully ask Jesus to show you what He wants you to learn from them:

"I am the good shepherd. The good shepherd lays down his life for the sheep." (John 10:11 NIV)

"He tends his flock like a shepherd: He gathers the lambs in his arms and carries them close to his heart; he gently leads those that have young." (Isaiah 40:11 NIV)

"My sheep listen to my voice; I know them, and they follow me. I give them eternal life, and they shall never perish; no one will snatch them out of my hand. My Father, who has given them to me, is greater than all; no one can snatch them out of my Father's hand." (John 10:27–29 NIV)

- A good shepherd protects, feeds, and cares for his sheep. When we stay close to the Shepherd, He leads us to the right places. When we wander off, we can get lost, hurt, and confused. But Jesus always comes for us. Matthew 18:12 (NIV) says: "What do you think? If a man owns a hundred sheep, and one of them wanders away, will he not leave the ninety-nine on the hills and go to look for the one that wandered off?" Where are you feeling lost, hurt, or confused? Ask the Good Shepherd to come for you.

- Commit to staying close to your Shepherd, Jesus. He will always lead you on the right path. He will refresh and restore your life. Pray that God continues to make His voice known to you.

....

Jesus, You are my gentle Shepherd. You are my wise and kind Leader. I know You care for me and You want me to know Your voice. Help me follow close to You. Lead me on the right paths as I stick close by.

Scripture Prayer Map

*O give thanks to the LORD, call on His name; make His
deeds known among the peoples. Sing to Him, sing
praises to Him; speak of all His wonders. Glory in His
holy name; let the hearts of those who seek the LORD
rejoice. Seek the LORD and His strength; seek His face
continually [longing to be in His presence].*

1 CHRONICLES 16:8–11 AMP

- We're going to use today's scripture as a map
  for prayer. The first line is *"O give thanks
  to the LORD, call on His name."* Begin your
  prayer today in thanksgiving as you call on
  His name. Thank Him for anything and everything you can think of.

- *"Make His deeds known among the peoples."*
  Ask Jesus to bring someone to mind who
  needs to be reminded that they are loved.
  Pray for them. Ask God if He wants you to
  reach out to that person in some way.

- *"Sing to Him, sing praises to Him."* Put on your
  favorite worship music and pray to Him in
  song.

- *"Speak of all His wonders."* As you're praying,
  thank God for the wonders you've seen Him
  do. They can be everyday miracles in your
  life, the miracles of creation that you've

witnessed, friends and family coming to Christ, etc. Thank God for all of that. Write them down in your prayer journal.

- *"Glory in His holy name."* According to *Strong's* concordance, "to glory" means "to boast, to praise, to celebrate." How can you celebrate and boast about God's name today? Ask Him what He would love for you to do.

- *"Let the hearts of those who seek the Lord rejoice."* Let your heart rejoice as you pray. Where are you finding joy in your life and your relationship with God? Tell Him.

- *"Seek the Lord and His strength."* As you seek the Lord in prayer, ask Him to fill you with His strength for your day. Where do you need His power to show up in your life today?

- *"Seek His face continually [longing to be in His presence]."* Ask for God to help you seek Him in all things. Ask Him to give you a desire and a longing for His presence.

....

Lord, I'm so thankful for Your words to inspire me as I talk with You. Please give me a deep desire and a longing to know You more and to spend time with You in Your Word and in prayer.

Fully Clothed and Well Prepared

*Then He opened their minds to [help them] understand
the Scriptures, and said, "And so it is written, that
the Christ (the Messiah, the Anointed) would suffer
and rise from the dead on the third day, and that
repentance [necessary] for forgiveness of sins would
be preached in His name to all the nations, beginning
from Jerusalem. You are witnesses of these things.
Listen carefully: I am sending the Promise of My Father
[the Holy Spirit] upon you; but you are to remain
in the city [of Jerusalem] until you are clothed
(fully equipped) with power from on high."*

LUKE 24:45–49 AMP

- Jesus promised us His Holy Spirit to comfort us, teach us, and remind us of everything that Jesus told us. He is the power that is alive in your heart the moment you invite Jesus to be your Lord and Savior. Have you done this already? Thank God for His great gift for you! If you haven't, what's stopping you? Do you want His love and supernatural power to lead and guide you? The greatest adventure of your life is living in a loving relationship with your Creator. Commit your life to Him today!

- To repent of your sins means that you ask Jesus for His forgiveness of any wrongdoing, you change your mind about the wrong behavior, and you choose to avoid that sin in the future. Do you need to repent of any sins in your life? Ask the Holy Spirit to give you the power you need to change your actions.

- With the Holy Spirit alive in your heart, you are fully clothed and fully equipped with power from God! Think about everything you've got going on in your life. Where do you need to be more fully equipped with the power of God? Ask for God to pour His power into your life through the Holy Spirit.

....

Lord Jesus, please open my mind to understand Your words. Thank You for the promise of Your Holy Spirit. I invite You to be Lord of my life and to pour Your mighty resurrection power into my life on a daily basis. I ask forgiveness for all the times I've messed up. Your Word tells me that Your sacrifice on the cross covers those sins and makes me clean before You. Thank You, Jesus!

Praying for Leaders and Others

Every time we think of you, we thank God for you.
Day and night you're in our prayers as we call to
mind your work of faith, your labor of love, and your
patience of hope in following our Master, Jesus Christ,
before God our Father. It is clear to us, friends,
that God not only loves you very much but also has
put his hand on you for something special. When the
Message we preached came to you, it wasn't just
words. Something happened in you. The Holy
Spirit put steel in your convictions.

1 THESSALONIANS 1:2–5 MSG

- Whenever God brings someone to your mind, pray for them. The Bible tells us that our prayers are powerful. We don't exactly know the miracles that take place when we pray, but we do know that God hears and always answers with a yes, a no, or a "not yet." The Bible also tells us that sometimes angels are given assignments when we pray (Psalm 91:11; Daniel 9:23; Daniel 10:11–12). Who is coming to your mind right now? Lift them up in prayer.

- Pray for your world leaders. First Timothy 2:1–2 (NLT) says: "I urge you, first of all, to pray for all people. Ask God to help them; intercede on their behalf, and give thanks for them. Pray this way for kings and all who are in authority so that we can live peaceful and quiet lives marked by godliness and dignity."

- Pray for your local leaders and the people that have personal leadership in your life, such as parents, teachers, youth group leaders, and pastors. Pray for blessing over their lives and families. Pray that they would lead well from a pure heart. Pray that they would be good listeners and be humble in heart. Pray that they would grow in their love for Jesus and others.

- God has put His hand on you for something special. With the very Spirit of God alive and at work in you, you are capable of anything! Commit your plans and your life to Him. Ask God to lead you as you follow His will for your life and become the kind of leader He wants you to be.

....

God, please bring to mind anyone who needs me to pray for them today. I don't completely understand the mystery of prayer, but I know it's powerful, and I take it seriously.

Faith

*Now faith is the assurance of things hoped for, the
conviction of things not seen. For by it the people
of old received their commendation. By faith we
understand that the universe was created by the
word of God, so that what is seen was not made out
of things that are visible. . . . And without faith it is
impossible to please him, for whoever would draw
near to God must believe that he exists and
that he rewards those who seek him.*

Hebrews 11:1–3, 6 esv

- *The Message* translation of Hebrews 11:6 says:
  "It's impossible to please God apart from
  faith. And why? Because anyone who wants
  to approach God must believe both that he
  exists and that he cares enough to respond
  to those who seek him." Is your faith pleasing to God? Do you believe that He cares
  enough to respond to you when you seek
  Him? Talk to Him about this.

- Faith is believing in the unseen. It's trusting
  that God is real and that He is alive and working in our lives. Ask God to deepen your faith.
  Mark 9:24 (niv) says: "I do believe; help me
  overcome my unbelief!" This is a valid prayer.
  Ask Jesus to help you overcome any unbelief
  you have in your heart.

- Have you believed anything that is untrue about God? Maybe your secret thoughts or actions tell a different story than what you profess to believe to your friends or family? Ask God to show you the truth in this area. Do you really trust that God can do anything? Or do your thoughts and actions actually show that you believe God to be powerless in some areas of your life and you need to take care of some things alone? Confess these beliefs to God. Ask for His help in believing the truth.

- Sometimes it's easier to believe in people and programs at church than in a God we can't physically see. When that happens, those people and programs become idols that can take the place of God. Repent of those beliefs and ask God to remove any idols in your heart.

....

God, I want my faith to be pleasing to You. Forgive me for the times I've believed that You are powerless in certain areas and that I have to do things all by myself. Help my unbelief. Please increase my faith.

The Great Exchange

*But he said to me, "My grace is sufficient for you,
for my power is made perfect in weakness." Therefore I
will boast all the more gladly about my weaknesses,
so that Christ's power may rest on me. That is why,
for Christ's sake, I delight in weaknesses, in insults,
in hardships, in persecutions, in difficulties.
For when I am weak, then I am strong.*

2 CORINTHIANS 12:9–10 NIV

- God likes to exchange things: old for new, death for life, ashes for beauty, sadness for joy, despair for praise (see Isaiah 61:3). He also exchanges our weakness for His strength. When those of us who are weak are able to do something in the obvious power of Christ alone, He is glorified and people take notice. What do you need God to exchange for you today? Ask Him.

- Bring all your weaknesses to Jesus and lay them at His feet. Can you picture yourself doing that? What does Jesus have to say to you? Ask for Him to exchange your weaknesses for His power.

- First Corinthians 1:25 (NIV) says: "For the foolishness of God is wiser than human wisdom, and the weakness of God is stronger than human strength." God is beyond our understanding. His strength is beyond compare. Praise God in prayer for His mighty strength and power. Thank Him for defeating death, the ultimate weakness. Praise Him for exchanging death for life.

- Hebrews 4:15–16 (MSG) says: "He's been through weakness and testing, experienced it all—all but the sin. So let's walk right up to him and get what he is so ready to give. Take the mercy, accept the help." Because of Jesus, you have the ability to walk right up to God and talk to Him. He is so ready to help you exchange the bad for the good.

. . . .

God, I'm so thankful that You can turn my darkness into light, my sadness into joy, my ashes into beauty, and my weakness into Your strength. You have forever defeated death and given me eternal life instead. I bring You my weaknesses. I lay them down at Your feet and ask that You would fill me with Your supernatural strength and power. Not so that I can get all the glory, but so that You can. I love You, Lord.

The End of the Rope

Hurry with your answer, GOD! I'm nearly at the end of my rope. Don't turn away; don't ignore me! That would be certain death. If you wake me each morning with the sound of your loving voice, I'll go to sleep each night trusting in you. Point out the road I must travel; I'm all ears, all eyes before you. Save me from my enemies, GOD—you're my only hope! Teach me how to live to please you, because you're my God. Lead me by your blessed Spirit into cleared and level pastureland. Keep up your reputation, God—give me life! In your justice, get me out of this trouble! In your great love, vanquish my enemies; make a clean sweep of those who harass me. And why? Because I'm your servant.

PSALM 143:7–12 MSG

- A wise youth speaker once said, "The end of your rope is God's permanent address." When you get to the end of your rope, you realize that all your efforts to save yourself have failed. You need Jesus. He's there. He's waiting. Are you or a friend struggling with depression? Cry out to God for help. He's waiting.

- The psalms are full of gut-wrenchingly honest prayers. God can handle your honesty. He knows exactly how you're feeling. He knows exactly what you need. Tell Him what you need Him to know. Share your heart.

- Bring to mind any friends or family members who seem sad, lonely, or depressed. Lift them before the God who cares for them and loves them deeply. Ask that they will be comforted and that their eyes and hearts would be open to the love of God.

- Psalm 40:1–2 (NLT) says: "I waited patiently for the LORD to help me, and he turned to me and heard my cry. He lifted me out of the pit of despair, out of the mud and the mire. He set my feet on solid ground and steadied me as I walked along." Use this scripture as your prayer. Ask God to steady you and set your feet on solid ground.

....

Jesus, when my heart is full of sadness and loneliness, I cry out to You. I believe that You care for me. Please fill me with hope. Not only the hope of heaven, but hope for the here and now. I lift my friends and family to You also. They need Your healing touch.

Relationships Matter

*Do a favor and win a friend forever; nothing can untie
that bond. Words satisfy the mind as much as fruit
does the stomach; good talk is as gratifying as a good
harvest. Words kill, words give life; they're either
poison or fruit—you choose. Find a good spouse, you
find a good life—and even more: the favor of God!
The poor speak in soft supplications; the rich bark
out answers. Friends come and friends go,
but a true friend sticks by you like family.*

PROVERBS 18:19–24 MSG

- Your friendships are important to God. Pray for God to be honored in your friendships. Ask Him to help you make wise decisions when you're with your friends. Pray for courage to share what God is speaking to your heart when you and your friends are talking.

- Bring each of your close friends to mind. Lift each of them up to God. Ask God to bless them with His love, comfort, and protection.

- The Bible has a lot to say about the kinds of friends we pick. Proverbs 22:24–25 (NLT) says: "Don't befriend angry people or associate with hot-tempered people, or you will learn to be like them and endanger your soul." Ask God to bring good, loving people into your life. Pray and ask that God will help you set up healthy boundaries with your friends.

- Your friends don't define you, and they don't get to tell you who you are. God is the only One who has the right to tell you who you are because He made you. Ask God to strengthen your confidence of who you are in Christ. Remember that list of truths you prayed about earlier in the book (pages 32–33)? Say a few of these truths out loud as you pray today. Ask for God to solidify them in your heart and mind:

- I am free and clean in the blood of Christ.
- I am a precious child of the Father.
- He delights in me.
- I am a friend of Christ.
- Nothing can separate me from God's love.
- God sees me as beautiful, and I am wonderfully made.
- God is for me, not against me.

....

Lord, thank You for my friends. Please help me make wise decisions when I'm with them. Remind me of who I am in You and of the courage that gives me to share the truth about You.

A Safe Place

Therefore let all the faithful pray to you while you may be found; surely the rising of the mighty waters will not reach them. You are my hiding place; you will protect me from trouble and surround me with songs of deliverance. I will instruct you and teach you in the way you should go; I will counsel you with my loving eye on you. . . . Many are the woes of the wicked, but the LORD's unfailing love surrounds the one who trusts in him. Rejoice in the LORD and be glad, you righteous; sing, all you who are upright in heart!

PSALM 32:6–8, 10–11 NIV

- God wants you to talk to Him. He wants to be found by you. He is a personal God longing for you to know His heart. Pray and ask God to show you a piece of His heart that you didn't know or understand before.

- God is our hiding place. When you feel like running away from the world, you can run to Jesus. He will protect you and show you which way to go next. He is your very own personal Christian counselor. Imagine yourself in a counselor's office. What would you tell the counselor? Can you picture Jesus sitting in the chair? The Bible tells us that He counsels us and watches over us lovingly. Tell Him everything you would say to the counselor. What does Jesus want you to know? Ask Him to show you.

- Do you feel surrounded by the unfailing love of God? Why or why not? His love for you never changes, and there is nothing you can do to earn it. Sometimes our own mental blocks get in the way and prevent us from knowing and feeling the truth. Is there anything you need to confess or let go of so that you can feel His love? Ask God to show you anything that might be preventing you from knowing and believing His love. Picture Jesus wrapping His loving arms around you just like the psalms talk about.

....

Thank You for being a safe place for me to hide, Lord. I ask You to wrap Your loving arms around me. Thank You for being my Counselor and always giving me the guidance I need when I come to You and ask. I know the truth of Your unfailing love. Please let that head knowledge move to heart knowledge.

Taking Your Thoughts Captive

*For though we live in the world, we do not wage war
as the world does. The weapons we fight with are not
the weapons of the world. On the contrary, they have
divine power to demolish strongholds. We demolish
arguments and every pretension that sets itself up
against the knowledge of God, and we take captive
every thought to make it obedient to Christ.*

2 Corinthians 10:3–5 niv

- As a child of God, remember that you have
  spiritual armor (Ephesians 6:10–18). These are
  the weapons God has given you to protect
  you from being sucked in by the thoughts
  and actions of this world. This world is a
  beautiful place, created by God. But there
  is also a darkness lurking that can easily
  become a major distraction. Selfishness and
  personal pleasure are part of this darkness.
  Pray and ask God to protect you from the
  darkness and temptations of today's culture.
  Picture yourself putting on the whole armor
  of God.

- Ask God for help to live in this world but
  not be *of* it (John 17:14–16). This means that
  we don't have the same value system as the
  people of the world who aren't following

Jesus. We're supposed to be different! Being different is good. Pray and ask God for the courage to be different.

- Pray for supernatural power to take your thoughts captive. You are preparing for the war in your mind that affects everything you do. Taking your thoughts captive means that you are training your brain to take the impure thoughts that will come to mind and switch them to good ones. This takes practice and prayer. Ask for help.

- Philippians 4:8 (NIV) says: "Finally, brothers and sisters, whatever is true, whatever is noble, whatever is right, whatever is pure, whatever is lovely, whatever is admirable—if anything is excellent or praiseworthy—think about such things." Ask God to help you memorize one of the verses from today's prayer plan. The Holy Spirit is with you to help you remember this verse and bring it to mind at just the right time when you need it the most.

....

God, I'm so thankful for the spiritual armor You have given me. Strengthen me and train me to take my thoughts captive. I'm going to need Your supernatural power to succeed in this. Thank You for being with me!

Be an Open Book with God

*GOD, investigate my life; get all the facts firsthand.
I'm an open book to you; even from a distance,
you know what I'm thinking. You know when I leave
and when I get back; I'm never out of your sight.
You know everything I'm going to say before I start
the first sentence. I look behind me and you're
there, then up ahead and you're there, too—your
reassuring presence, coming and going.*

PSALM 139:1-5 MSG

- We're going to focus on opening up to God today. Can you quiet your heart and mind before God? Go to a quiet place, or if you can't find a quiet place, imagine one in your head. Imagine a safe and peaceful place. Maybe the beach or a forest, or beside a river. Picture yourself there and invite Jesus in. Ask Him to sit beside you. Do you have that picture in your mind?

- Go beyond a conversation with a friend and remind yourself that you're sharing with the One who will never betray you. Your words and thoughts are completely safe with Him. You can be completely open. Ask Him to take a look inside your heart and mind. What does He want to talk with you about?

- God wants to fill us with His love and His truth. He wants to remove any lies we believe so that we can walk in the light of His truth. John 8:32 (NIV) tells us: "Then you will know the truth, and the truth will set you free." Picture yourself as an open book before Jesus. What truth does He want you to know?

- You are never out of God's sight. He knows what you're going to say before you even say it. But still, He wants to talk with you. He wants to know your heart, and He wants you to know His. Ask God to give you a deep desire and longing to get closer with Him every day.

....

Jesus, please remove any fears in my heart about letting You into the deepest parts of me. Your Word tells me that perfect love casts out fear (1 John 4:18) and that I don't have to be afraid that I'll be punished for any of my thoughts. You see them, and You want to tell me the truth about what I'm thinking and feeling. I invite You in to do that, Lord.

Unity and Maturity

We are glad when we are weak [since God's power comes freely through us], but you [by comparison] are strong. We also pray for this, that you be made complete [fully restored, growing and maturing in godly character and spirit—pleasing your heavenly Father by the life you live]. . . . Finally, believers, rejoice! Be made complete [be what you should be], be comforted, be like-minded, live in peace [enjoy the spiritual well-being experienced by believers who walk closely with God]; and the God of love and peace [the source of lovingkindness] will be with you.

2 CORINTHIANS 13:9, 11 AMP

- Paul and his followers were praying for the Corinthians, and we should pray similarly for our brothers and sisters in Christ. Take some time and pray for your church and for other churches you're familiar with around the world. Pray that the message of Christ will be taught clearly and truthfully.

- Does your church support any missionaries? Pray for them, even if you don't know their names. Ephesians 6:19 (NIV) says: "Pray also for me, that whenever I speak, words may be given me so that I will fearlessly make known the mystery of the gospel." Pray that they would share the love of Jesus without fear.

Pray for their protection as they share the Gospel in foreign lands. Pray for unity with the missionaries on their teams.

- Pray specifically for your church and any ministry teams that you belong to. Pray for your youth group. Ask God to bring unity to the teams you are a part of. Ask Him to help the leaders grow and mature in godly character. Pray for peace and joy to be known and felt at your church.

- These verses apply to you as well. As you end your prayer time, ask God to complete the work He started in you (Philippians 1:6). Ask Him to help you grow in maturity and godly character. Pray that He helps you have courage to share the love of Jesus with the people in your life.

....

Lord, I lift up my fellow believers around the world. Help us live authentic and loving lives based on the truth of Your Word. I pray for the missionaries I know. Keep them safe, and give them joy and peace as they share the Gospel.

Big People, Small God

The LORD is my light and my salvation—whom shall I fear? The LORD is the stronghold of my life—of whom shall I be afraid? . . . One thing I ask from the LORD, this only do I seek: that I may dwell in the house of the LORD all the days of my life, to gaze on the beauty of the LORD and to seek him in his temple. For in the day of trouble he will keep me safe in his dwelling; he will hide me in the shelter of his sacred tent and set me high upon a rock.

PSALM 27:1, 4–5 NIV

- When people are bigger and more important in your life, God's power can seem smaller and unavailable to you. The Bible tells us that the fear of God is the beginning of wisdom (Proverbs 9:10). That doesn't mean we are afraid to approach God. No! Nothing could be further from the truth. We are able to boldly go into God's presence because of Jesus (Ephesians 3:12; Hebrews 4:16). But fearing God more than people means that we honor our holy and powerful God and we have no other idols before Him. We don't put other people in God's place. Ask for God to search your heart again today. Is there anything or any person you need to lay down before God so that He can take His rightful spot in your life?

- People can seem downright scary sometimes. An angry kid at school. A teacher you have trouble with. A bully. Even though being around that person might feel intimidating, remember that God is bigger! Trust that God has all the power and that when you bring that person before God, He can help! Bring to mind any person in your life that makes you a little bit scared. Ask God to protect you. Ask Him to give you His perspective of that person.

- Remember that God is our safe hiding place. When you are afraid of anything, you can always run to Him for help and safety. What are you feeling scared of today? Bring it to Jesus in prayer.

....

Lord, please make it my heart's desire to be in Your safe and loving presence for the rest of my life. Please remove any idols I've put ahead of You. Remind me that You are bigger than any person.

Children of Light

The true light that gives light to everyone was coming into the world. He was in the world, and though the world was made through him, the world did not recognize him. He came to that which was his own, but his own did not receive him. Yet to all who did receive him, to those who believed in his name, he gave the right to become children of God—children born not of natural descent, nor of human decision or a husband's will, but born of God.

JOHN 1:9–13 NIV

- Do these verses from John sound familiar in the world we live in today? The true light came into the world. That light was actually the God who made everything. But the world didn't recognize Him. When you are born of God, that light lives in you. Our dark world can be a hostile place for those trying to shine the light. Is that something you sense and feel on a regular basis? John 8:12 (ESV) says: "Again Jesus spoke to them, saying, 'I am the light of the world. Whoever follows me will not walk in darkness, but will have the light of life.'" Pray that God will help you live in the light. Ask Him to help you shine your light in dark places. Ask Him for protection as you do that.

- Ephesians 5:8 (ESV) says: "For at one time you were darkness, but now you are light in the Lord. Walk as children of light." First Thessalonians 5:5 (ESV) tells us the same thing: "For you are all children of light, children of the day." Get in the habit of thinking of yourself in this way. You are a child of God, a child of light. Ask the Holy Spirit to remind you of this and for help in accepting this as truth in your heart. Picture yourself bringing God's light into dark places. Ask for His guidance as you walk as a child of light.

- You are born of God—His beloved creation. Tell God how this makes you feel. Praise Him for His goodness. Thank Him for equipping you to live as light in this world.

....

Light of the World, thank You for planting Your light in my heart. Remind me that I'm Your beloved child, a child of light. Help me walk in Your ways and carry Your light with me wherever I go.

Light Overcomes the Darkness

*In the beginning the Word already existed. The Word
was with God, and the Word was God. He existed
in the beginning with God. God created everything
through him, and nothing was created except through
him. The Word gave life to everything that was
created, and his life brought light to everyone.
The light shines in the darkness, and the
darkness can never extinguish it.*

JOHN 1:1–5 NLT

- We're going to pray more about the light
of Jesus today. Jesus gives us tons of visual
imagery in His teachings. In Matthew 5:14–16
(NIV), He says, "You are the light of the world.
A town built on a hill cannot be hidden. Neither do people light a lamp and put it under
a bowl. Instead they put it on its stand, and
it gives light to everyone in the house. In the
same way, let your light shine before others,
that they may see your good deeds and
glorify your Father in heaven." Picture this
in your mind as you pray. Ask Jesus to help
you shine your light to brighten up the world
around you.

- Use this verse as a prayer guide: "But you are
a chosen people, a royal priesthood, a holy

nation, God's special possession, that you may declare the praises of him who called you out of darkness into his wonderful light" (1 Peter 2:9 NIV). Ask God to tell you who you are to Him. How does God feel about you? Ask Him to show you. Praise Him for bringing you out of darkness and into His light.

- The life of Jesus brought light to us. God's Word tells us that the darkness can never put out the light. That's a promise. Thank God for that promise. Pray that God would help you bring that powerful light into a dark world. Ask for boldness, strength, and guidance.

....

You are not a created being, God. You always were and always will be. That's hard to wrap my brain around sometimes. But I believe what You've said. I believe You are the light that has brought me out of darkness. I'm Your chosen daughter. You thought of me before the creation of the world. Thank You for Your promise that the darkness can never extinguish the light. Fill me with Your light so that I can make a difference in a dark world.

Praying for Strength

Now to Him who is able to establish and strengthen you [in the faith] according to my gospel and the preaching of Jesus Christ, according to the revelation of the mystery [of the plan of salvation] which has been kept secret for long ages past, but now has been disclosed and through the prophetic Scriptures has been made known to all the nations, according to the commandment of the eternal God, leading them to obedience to the faith, to the only wise God, through Jesus Christ, be the glory forevermore! Amen.

ROMANS 16:25–27 AMP

- Jesus is able to strengthen and establish you (1 Peter 5:10). He is the author and perfecter of our faith (Hebrews 12:2). Some translations say He is the founder and finisher of our faith. He will finish what He started in you (Philippians 1:6). Thank God for the faith He has given you. Ask Him to increase your faith as He finishes and perfects the good work He began in you.

- When you are feeling weak and tired, ask God for help. Pray that He will fill you with His life and a renewed energy to do the work He has for you to do today, whether it's school, family responsibilities, chores, youth group, etc.

- When you are feeling weak in your faith and are worried that you might cave to peer pressure, pray for God to intervene on your behalf. Thank God for the promise that He'll always provide a way out for you. First Corinthians 10:13 (NIV) says: "No temptation has overtaken you except what is common to mankind. And God is faithful; he will not let you be tempted beyond what you can bear. But when you are tempted, he will also provide a way out so that you can endure it." Ask the Holy Spirit to help you remember this verse!

....

Thank You, Lord, for my faith. I'm glad I'm Your child and that You've filled me with Your life and hope. I pray for strength to endure whatever comes my way and for the energy to get the things done that I need to. I trust that You'll finish the work You've started in me. Please strengthen my faith, especially when it comes to temptation. Please show me the way out when I need it.

Accountability and Prayer

*Therefore, confess your sins to one another [your false
steps, your offenses], and pray for one another,
that you may be healed and restored. The heartfelt
and persistent prayer of a righteous man (believer)
can accomplish much [when put into action and
made effective by God—it is dynamic and
can have tremendous power].*

JAMES 5:16 AMP

- Prayer is very powerful. The Bible tells us
  so! Your prayers matter to God, and they
  can accomplish a lot. God's Word tells us to
  pray for others so that they can be healed
  and restored. This is not only referring to
  physical bodies being healed and restored,
  but also hearts and minds being healed and
  made whole. Are you in the habit of praying
  for restoration? Who in your life needs to be
  restored and made whole? Bring them before
  God in prayer.

- Confessing your sins to someone else and
  having them hold you accountable in faith
  and life goals is a great way to grow in maturity. Hebrews 10:24–25 (NIV) says: "And let us
  consider how we may spur one another on
  toward love and good deeds, not giving up

meeting together, as some are in the habit of doing, but encouraging one another—and all the more as you see the Day approaching." Do you have an accountability partner or mentor? Talk to God about this. Is this something you feel Him stirring in your heart?

- An accountability partner needs to be a safe person who will keep your thoughts and feelings to herself. This person should be dependable so that you can plan on meeting together regularly. This person should also love God and desire to follow His will for her life. Make a list of several godly girls or older women who come to mind. Pray for God to direct you to a trustworthy person who can encourage you and help you grow in faith.

....

Thank You that my prayers matter to You, God! Please show me if You'd like me to get together with another believer to encourage and grow in our faith. Put the right person in my path so that we can form a healthy bond as we share each other's burdens, prayer requests, and life goals.

Gossip or Goodness

Sunrise breaks through the darkness for good people—
God's grace and mercy and justice! The good person is
generous and lends lavishly; no shuffling or stumbling
around for this one, but a sterling and solid and lasting
reputation. Unfazed by rumor and gossip, heart ready,
trusting in GOD, spirit firm, unperturbed, ever blessed,
relaxed among enemies, they lavish gifts on
the poor—a generosity that goes on, and on,
and on. An honored life! A beautiful life!

PSALM 112:4–9 MSG

- As a teen girl, it's important to have a good
  reputation, right? You probably want to be
  known as a smart, kind, and respectful person
  who loves God. It's okay to want a good
  reputation, but what really matters is what
  God thinks of you. Sometimes rumors will
  go around about you that aren't true. If that
  happens, don't worry. Pray and ask God to
  help the truth come to light.

- Gossip hurts people. Take some time to look
  up the following scriptures about gossip:
  Proverbs 10:18–19; Proverbs 11:9, 13; Proverbs
  16:28; Proverbs 17:9; Proverbs 18:21. Bottom
  line? Gossip is wrong. But sometimes it's so
  hard to avoid when friends get together. Ask

God to forgive you for the times when you've participated. Ask God for strength and creativity to do the right thing when someone around you starts gossiping. You can change the subject, you can walk away, or you can ask them to stop. Ask God to give you the right words to say.

- Proverbs 20:19 (NIV) says: "A gossip betrays a confidence; so avoid anyone who talks too much." Ask God to help you honor this verse. Ask for wisdom to find good friends and avoid getting entangled with gossips.

- Let this be your prayer as you end today's thoughts: "Set a guard over my mouth, LORD; keep watch over the door of my lips" (Psalm 141:3 NIV).

. . . .

Thank You for my beautiful life, Lord. You have blessed me abundantly, and I'm so thankful. I want to honor You in my relationships and conversations. I'm young, and I make mistakes sometimes in this area, but I know You are with me and that You forgive and redirect me. I ask You for wisdom to know what to do when I'm with friends who are gossiping.

When You Don't Know
What to Pray

Meanwhile, the moment we get tired in the waiting,
God's Spirit is right alongside helping us along. If we
don't know how or what to pray, it doesn't matter.
He does our praying in and for us, making prayer out
of our wordless sighs, our aching groans. He knows
us far better than we know ourselves. . .and keeps
us present before God. That's why we can be
so sure that every detail in our lives of love
for God is worked into something good.

ROMANS 8:26–28 MSG

- There are days when you don't feel like praying. Maybe you've had a really bad week. Maybe you're sad. Maybe you're mad at people or even at God. You're not alone. Jesus is very aware of the human condition because He became one of us. God knows how you feel, and He knows that you are human with human understanding and feelings. That's why He's sent His Spirit to live inside us. To encourage us always. And the Bible tells us that the Spirit of God will pray in us and for us when we don't know what to pray for. . .or when we just don't feel like it. If you are feeling this way today, just sit quietly somewhere and breathe. Ask the Holy Spirit to pray for you.

- In Psalm 46:10 (NIV), God says, "Be still, and know that I am God." Ask God to clear your mind. Focus your thoughts on Jesus. Just enjoy being in His presence without saying a word.

- Are you in the middle of a difficult situation? Are you battling thoughts in your mind or dealing with a real-life problem? Exodus 14:14 (NIV) says: "The LORD will fight for you; you need only to be still." Be still before God. Picture Jesus fighting your battle for you. Listen. What does Jesus want you to notice?

....

Father, there are days when I don't know what to pray for or how to even begin. I thank You for sending Your Spirit to pray for me. You knew how much I would need that. Focus my thoughts on You. Clear my mind of distractions. Help me learn how to be still in Your presence and know that You are a good and loving God who is fighting my battles.

A Good Listener

Don't fool yourself into thinking that you are a listener
when you are anything but, letting the Word go in
one ear and out the other. Act on what you hear!
Those who hear and don't act are like those who
glance in the mirror, walk away, and two minutes
later have no idea who they are, what they look like.

JAMES 1:22–24 MSG

- The Bible tells us that someone who is good
  at listening to God listens for His voice and
  then does what He says. Are you letting
  God's voice go in one ear and out the other?
  Talk to God about this. Confess the times
  that you haven't acted on what God has
  asked of you. Ask Him for help in putting His
  words and plans into action.

- Proverbs 3:5–6 (MSG) says: "Don't try to figure
  out everything on your own. Listen for GOD's
  voice in everything you do, everywhere you
  go; he's the one who will keep you on track."
  God wants you to be listening for His voice
  and following His ways. Remember that God
  confirms what He's saying to you. He doesn't
  make you guess, and what He says will always
  line up with His Word. Talk to God about this.
  Ask Him for help in getting to know His voice

really well. Ask for ears to hear, eyes to see, and a willingness to act.

- Practice listening with your prayer journal. Direct your thoughts to Jesus and His Word. Let Him lead and guide you to what He wants you to know today. Prayerfully write down all the ways He is directing you. It may be a special scripture or a worship song or a reminder of a message you heard at church. Then ask Him to confirm it. How does He want you to put this into action? Ask Him to reveal this to you.

....

Lord, I want to be a good listener and to put into action everything that I hear from You. I don't want to be someone who just says she's a Christian but lives a totally different way, apart from You. Please continue to help me know and hear Your voice. Your Word tells me that You really want me to be able to hear from You. I accept this truth! Help me hear and do as I follow You.

He Came to Help

"This is how much God loved the world: He gave his Son, his one and only Son. And this is why: so that no one need be destroyed; by believing in him, anyone can have a whole and lasting life. God didn't go to all the trouble of sending his Son merely to point an accusing finger, telling the world how bad it was. He came to help, to put the world right again."

JOHN 3:16-17 MSG

- There is a common misconception among unbelievers (and sometimes believers too!) that God came to spoil all the fun. Many TV shows portray God as an angry being in the sky who will make lightning strike if you are blatantly dishonoring Him. From a secular point of view, He is rarely portrayed as the good and loving God who came to save us from ourselves. What do you believe about God? Do you believe He gets angry with you? Prayerfully read the following scriptures and ask God to reveal His truth to you as you read: Psalm 145:8; Jeremiah 31:3; Romans 8:31; 2 Corinthians 5:21; Colossians 3:3. Ask God for help to believe that He sees you through the lens of Jesus. Confess any wrong thoughts you may have believed about God.

- Jesus didn't come to earth to point fingers at all the bad, make people feel shame, and then leave us to try to figure out how to be good. No! He came to help. He came to make us right with God so that when God looks at us, He sees the righteousness of Jesus. Through His life, death, and resurrection, Jesus took all our sin and shame and nailed it to the cross. His sacrifice paid the penalty once and for all (Hebrews 10:10). Do you believe this? Tell God how this makes you feel. Praise Him for His undeserved sacrifice!

....

God, I'm so thankful that I can walk right up to You and boldly come into Your presence because of Jesus and His sacrifice for me. I am clean and perfect in Your sight because of the blood of Jesus. I want Him to fill me with His mighty resurrection power and life. Thank You for the cross, Lord. I won't take it for granted. Help me live my life in thanks.

Smarts about Social Media

Take no part in the worthless deeds of evil and darkness; instead, expose them. It is shameful even to talk about the things that ungodly people do in secret. But their evil intentions will be exposed when the light shines on them, for the light makes everything visible. This is why it is said, "Awake, O sleeper, rise up from the dead, and Christ will give you light." So be careful how you live. Don't live like fools, but like those who are wise. Make the most of every opportunity in these evil days. Don't act thoughtlessly, but understand what the Lord wants you to do.

EPHESIANS 5:11–17 NLT

- Look around at any time of day and you see just about everyone glued to their phones. There are many benefits of technology and social media, but there are also a lot of negatives. Does God care about your screen-time usage? You bet! Talk to Him about it. Ask Him to give you wisdom as you navigate social media.

- There are good things about social media. You can connect with friends and family you don't see very much or who live far away. There's a ton of good info out there, and inspiration for any project. Ask God for help to focus on the good and steer clear of the bad.

- There are negatives about social media too. There's a ton of darkness at your fingertips. People argue about everything. Posts and pictures of friends can make you feel sad and left out if you weren't invited. There's also a lot of temptation, including impure images and thoughts. Ask God to protect your heart and your mind when you're online. Ask Him to expose any lies you are believing because of things you've seen or read on social media.

- Screen time can easily take the place of God in our lives. Ask forgiveness if you need to for the amount of wasted time you've spent online. Ask God to help you with time management and focus.

- If you're going to post something, remember that you are God's representative. You can spread His kingdom online too. It's just like a mission field.

....

God, please help me not to put screen time ahead of You. I don't want it to be an idol that gets in the way of my relationship with You. Help me be wise online.

Stay Alert

Keep a cool head. Stay alert. The Devil is poised to pounce, and would like nothing better than to catch you napping. Keep your guard up. You're not the only ones plunged into these hard times. It's the same with Christians all over the world. So keep a firm grip on the faith. The suffering won't last forever. It won't be long before this generous God who has great plans for us in Christ—eternal and glorious plans they are!—will have you put together and on your feet for good. He gets the last word; yes, he does.

1 PETER 5:8–11 MSG

- The Bible tells us that we have an enemy. He is known as the father of lies (John 8:44), the accuser who discourages and condemns us (Revelation 12:10), and the ruler of darkness (Ephesians 6:12). Because of Jesus, the enemy can't take away your salvation (John 10:28), and he has been disarmed (Colossians 2:15). Even though the enemy knows he's been defeated, he's still trying his best to get into your head and discourage you so much you won't be able to live for Jesus. That's why Jesus wants you to stay alert. Are you believing any lies from the enemy right now? Are you discouraged or depressed? Pray and ask God to step in and reveal any lies of doubt and discouragement. Ask Him to fill your mind with the truth.

- Make a habit of putting on your armor daily. As you pray through the armor of God (see pages 18–19 or Ephesians 6:10–18), visualize Jesus placing this armor on you and preparing you to walk into battle.

- James 4:7 (AMP) says: "So submit to [the authority of] God. Resist the devil [stand firm against him] and he will flee from you." You have power in the name of Jesus to get rid of any evil you come up against. Thank God for this amazing truth!

- Remember, we focus on Jesus and His power to fight our battles! We don't focus on the fear of the enemy. Ask God to renew your strength and confidence in His ultimate power over everything.

....

Thanks again, Lord, for preparing me for life in a dark world. You have given me everything I need to win these battles in Your strength. Remove any fear that is lingering in my mind and fill me with Your truth.

Purity Online and IRL

The purpose of my instruction is that all believers would be filled with love that comes from a pure heart, a clear conscience, and genuine faith. But some people have missed this whole point. They have turned away from these things and spend their time in meaningless discussions.

1 TIMOTHY 1:5–6 NLT

- People were missing the point of Paul's message and spending their time in meaningless discussions and arguments. Paul's main goal as a missionary is stated here in 1 Timothy 1:5. He teaches so that all believers will be filled with love from a pure heart, clear conscience, and real-life faith. Pray about this. Ask God to purify your heart. Prayerfully read over Psalm 51. Ask God to cleanse you from sin.

- The Christian life is all about love from a pure heart. When it becomes more about rules and religion, that is not genuine faith in Christ. God's hope for you as a young person is that you'll be filled with purity and love. Psalm 119:9 (NIV) says: "How can a young person stay on the path of purity? By living according to your word." Ask Him to guard your heart online and IRL (in real life).

- Before you get online, ask God to cover you with His armor (see pages 18–19), specifically the helmet of salvation so that you remember that you are His and that you have the mind of Christ (1 Corinthians 2:16).

- Before you speak or post online, get in the habit of praying first. When you're in conversations with others IRL or online, say quick prayers in your mind and ask God to help you speak or post with love and wisdom. Ask God to help you steer clear of online arguments and meaningless conversations that cause division, hurt feelings, or gossip.

....

God, thank You that Your purpose for me is love and purity. Please guard my heart as I navigate relationships in a social-media culture. Fill me with Your love and presence. Please help me get in the habit of talking to You first before I post or get involved in conversations online or IRL. Remind me to speak truth in loving ways. I know I can't argue anyone into Your kingdom. That's pointless. Let me be known for comments and posts that point others to You from a mind and heart that's pure in my love for You and others.

Down to Earth

*When God, who is the best shepherd of all, comes
out in the open with his rule, he'll see that you've
done it right and commend you lavishly. And you who
are younger must follow your leaders. But all of you,
leaders and followers alike, are to be down to earth
with each other, for—God has had it with the proud,
but takes delight in just plain people. So be content
with who you are, and don't put on airs. God's strong
hand is on you; he'll promote you at the right time. Live
carefree before God; he is most careful with you.*

1 PETER 5:4–7 MSG

- Being down to earth means that you aren't
  prideful. You don't think you're better than
  everyone else. You live your life in reality, and
  you have common sense. Romans 12:3 (NLT)
  says: "Because of the privilege and authority
  God has given me, I give each of you this
  warning: Don't think you are better than you
  really are. Be honest in your evaluation of
  yourselves, measuring yourselves by the faith
  God has given us." Pray and ask for God to
  help you be more down to earth. Confess
  sins of pride or thinking higher of yourself
  than you ought to.

- It's okay to be confident in your skills and

giftedness. Maybe you're awesome at basketball or maybe you have a beautiful voice. God has given you those gifts for a purpose. But they can be used to bring Him glory or to bring glory to yourself. Which will you choose? Talk to God about that. Commit your gifts and abilities to God.

- God wants you to be content with who you are. He made you with all your uniqueness. You are absolutely beautiful in His sight, and He made you the way you are for a reason. Remember, these earthly bodies are only temporary. Thank God for the body He gave you, freckles and all!

....

Lord, help me embrace the body that You gave me, even the parts I have a hard time liking. I'm going to need Your power to do it. Help me not to compare what You've given me with what You've given others. I'm Your unique creation. Thank You for the skills I have. Help me sharpen them so they can be used to bring You glory.

Anxiety and Worry

"Therefore I tell you, do not be anxious about your life, what you will eat or what you will drink, nor about your body, what you will put on. Is not life more than food, and the body more than clothing? Look at the birds of the air: they neither sow nor reap nor gather into barns, and yet your heavenly Father feeds them. Are you not of more value than they? And which of you by being anxious can add a single hour to his span of life?"

MATTHEW 6:25–27 ESV

- Most girls tend to worry about so many things: hair, makeup, boys, clothes, school, sports. It's fun to do your best or get creative in those areas; the problem starts when they become an obsession. Talk to God about these things. Thank Him for them. Then lay them down before His throne. Confess if you've been obsessed with them at times. Ask God to give you a healthy view of these areas of your life.

- Read Matthew 6:28–30 during your prayer time. What does it say about how God clothes the flowers in the fields? Do you believe He cares about what you care about? Will He provide for you too? Confess your worry over these things to God. Ask Him to give you a right attitude about your clothes.

- Proverbs 12:25 (ESV) says: "Anxiety in a man's heart weighs him down, but a good word makes him glad." Did you know that anxiety and worry and obsession are actually bad for your body? It's a scientific fact that too much worry causes stress on your body, especially your heart, and can lead to disease and even death. Worry and anxiety mean that you're not trusting that God will take care of you. Bring your anxieties and worries to Jesus. Ask Him to exchange them for a confident trust in His power and care for you.

....

Jesus, please forgive me for worrying so much about things that won't last. Most of this stuff won't even matter ten years from now. Help me see the big picture. Please give me a healthy view of how I look and what I wear. Remind me that You will take care of me. Help me not to stress so much but to put my trust in You.

Worrying about Tomorrow

"But seek first his kingdom and his righteousness, and all these things will be given to you as well. Therefore do not worry about tomorrow, for tomorrow will worry about itself. Each day has enough trouble of its own."

MATTHEW 6:33–34 NIV

- If you are seeking God's kingdom and His will for your life, you will always be taken care of. You don't have to be afraid of the future. With God on your side and alive in your heart, you don't have to worry about tomorrow. Thank God for the life He's given you. Thank Him for always taking care of you and providing for you. Praise Him that you never have to be afraid of the future.

- Jeremiah 29:11 (NIV) is a scripture every teenager needs to commit to memory: " 'For I know the plans I have for you,' declares the LORD, 'plans to prosper you and not to harm you, plans to give you hope and a future.' " Pray and agree with this promise from God. Ask the Holy Spirit to help you remember it.

- Teenagers have to make a lot of important decisions every day. What classes to take, which colleges to look at, what job or internship to apply for. Stressing about those decisions doesn't have to be a part of your future. Philippians 4:19 (AMP) promises this: "And my God will liberally supply (fill until full) your every need according to His riches in glory in Christ Jesus." How cool is that? Thank Him for this promise too. Ask Him for peace and a calm spirit as you make decisions that affect your future. Ask Him for wisdom, knowing that He has you in the palm of His hand and is meeting your every need no matter what decision you make.

- Guess what? If you make a mistake or a wrong decision, God has your back. It's not the end of the world, so try not to stress. He can make crooked paths straight again (Proverbs 3:6). There is always a fresh start available and help to guide you on your way. Thank Him for His grace and love for you that covers all your mistakes. Ask for a fresh start if you need one.

....

Thank You that I don't have to stress over important decisions, Lord. You are with me, guiding me and giving me wisdom. I trust that You're holding me in Your hands.

Forgiveness

*Let all bitterness and wrath and anger and clamor
[perpetual animosity, resentment, strife, fault-finding]
and slander be put away from you, along with
every kind of malice [all spitefulness, verbal abuse,
malevolence]. Be kind and helpful to one another,
tender-hearted [compassionate, understanding],
forgiving one another [readily and freely],
just as God in Christ also forgave you.*

EPHESIANS 4:31-32 AMP

- We ask forgiveness from God when we sin because it breaks fellowship with Him. When we come to Him and confess our sins, our relationship is restored quickly. Is there any sin coming between you and God right now? Ask Him to search your heart.

- God wants us to forgive others just as quickly because when we carry around unforgiveness, it really gets in the way. Are there friends or family members who have wronged you recently? Ask God for help to forgive them. Have you hurt someone yourself? Go to them and make amends. Ask God for courage to do the right thing.

- Forgiveness and reconciliation are not the same thing. Reconciliation takes two people willing to repent and work out a problem God's way so that you can build trust for the future. If someone has wronged you severely, you are not required to trust that person again. But with God's help, you can forgive them. Forgiveness means you leave the judgment and punishment in God's hands. You don't seek your own revenge. You let it go, knowing that God is just. They will have to work at earning trust if you are to reconcile in the future. Ask God for help understanding this. Has anyone wronged you in this way? Pray about the situation. Ask for God's will to be done. Ask for His strength to forgive and the wisdom to know what to do next. Does God want this relationship to end, or is there hope of reconciliation? Ask Him to lead you.

....

Lord, help me forgive Your way—readily and freely—so I don't carry around a bunch of burdens that I'm not meant to carry. Help me be quick to admit when I've done wrong to others and do whatever I need to do to make things right when it's my fault. When I mess up, You readily forgive me. Help me do the same. Please give me wisdom in relationships where I've been hurt badly. Show me Your will and Your way.

Finding Rest

"Come to Me, all who are weary and heavily burdened [by religious rituals that provide no peace], and I will give you rest [refreshing your souls with salvation]. Take My yoke upon you and learn from Me [following Me as My disciple], for I am gentle and humble in heart, and you will find rest (renewal, blessed quiet) for your souls. For My yoke is easy [to bear] and My burden is light."

MATTHEW 11:28–30 AMP

- Are you feeling worn-out? Maybe school, friends, sports, or trying to make everyone else happy has you exhausted and ready to give up. Jesus invites you to come to Him to find the rest that you need. You don't have to do any work to receive His love and acceptance. Just be you and allow yourself to fall into His arms. Can you picture this? Ask Jesus to bring you comfort and rest.

- Studies show that teenagers need their rest! Your body and mind are growing fast, and growing is a lot of work, which means sleep is crucial. Thank God for your growing body. Ask Him for help and wisdom to get the amount of sleep your body needs to be healthy. He cares about your health.

- Jesus talks about a different kind of rest. He gives rest to the soul as well as the body. A deep soul rest is the kind you need when you're exhausted from trying to make everyone happy. God doesn't want you to take all that on yourself. Come to Him. Bring Him your thoughts and feelings. Allow Him to give your soul and mind a rest.

- *The Message* translation of today's verses says: "Come to me. Get away with me and you'll recover your life. . . . I won't lay anything heavy or ill-fitting on you. Keep company with me and you'll learn to live freely and lightly." Doesn't that sound amazing? Ask Jesus to help you live freely and lightly. He alone can give you the true rest that you need.

. . . .

Your promise sounds so great to me, Jesus. And I believe it's true. I need the rest You are offering. I bring my soul to You. Please refresh it. Fill me with Your love and a renewed strength that comes from being with You. I want to recover my life. Show me how to live freely and lightly without trying to please everyone else.

Money and Generosity

*Tell those rich in this world's wealth to quit being so
full of themselves and so obsessed with money, which
is here today and gone tomorrow. Tell them to go
after God, who piles on all the riches we could ever
manage—to do good, to be rich in helping others, to be
extravagantly generous. If they do that, they'll build
a treasury that will last, gaining life that is truly life.*

1 TIMOTHY 6:17–19 MSG

- These verses in *The Message* translation of
  the Bible really tell it like it is! Having lots of
  money and getting more money is the number one priority on many people's list. What
  about yours? Do you find yourself wishing
  you had a lot more money than you do? Do
  you keep wishing for more and more stuff?
  Ask God to change your desires to match His.
  There's nothing wrong with making a good
  wage for your efforts. Ask God to instill a
  healthy view of money in your heart.

- God wants us to run after Him, not money
  and things that don't last. But many people your age chase after all kinds of stuff:
  money, clothes, electronics, and a lot of other
  "things" that don't really matter. But here's
  the truth: Chasing after all of that will never

fill you up and make you truly happy. Only God can meet the deep longings in your heart. During your prayer time, take a look at Matthew 6. Read all of it if you have time, or just little chunks over the next few days. Ask the Holy Spirit to make Jesus' words come alive to you. What does He want you to do about this?

- Ask God to plant seeds of generosity in your heart. Listen up at church and in your community for needs that you and your family might be able to meet financially. Ask God to make you extra generous with what you already have and for a giving heart.

....

God, forgive me for the times I can only think about getting more. I don't want to live like that. Help me be content with what I have. Please give me a generous heart where I think of others and their needs before my own. Help me be on the lookout for needs around me that I might be able to meet. Remind me that everything I have belongs to You anyway.

Clothes That Matter

Since God chose you to be the holy people he loves,
you must clothe yourselves with tenderhearted mercy,
kindness, humility, gentleness, and patience.
Make allowance for each other's faults, and forgive
anyone who offends you. Remember, the Lord forgave
you, so you must forgive others. Above all,
clothe yourselves with love, which binds
us all together in perfect harmony.

COLOSSIANS 3:12–14 NLT

- You might know some girls who spend a lot of time putting outfits together. You might be one of them! Designing outfits and coordinating accessories can be a lot of fun. In fact, God put those kinds of desires and skills and giftedness inside you for a purpose. Maybe you'll be a stylist someday and you can use those gifts to further God's kingdom. Thank God for providing for you in this way. Thank Him that you have so many clothes to wear. Many kids your age in other countries barely have enough clothing to change their outfits at all. Pray for them to find the help they need. Ask God to show you how you can help. Can you share some of your excess with those in need? Talk to Jesus about this.

- The Bible talks about a different kind of clothes—spiritual clothes like mercy, kindness, humility, gentleness, patience, and forgiveness. When you're putting on the armor of God for protection each day, ask God to clothe you with these spiritual clothes too. That can seem like a lot to remember, and God knows that. That's why He said if you can't remember to wear anything else, wear love. Love is the most important. Because if you are loving God and loving others, everything else will automatically fall into place. Ask God to help you get in the habit of "wearing" love every day.

- Forgiveness is so important to God (Matthew 6:14–15). You'll have to do a lot of it in your lifetime if you want to live "freely and lightly" (Matthew 11:30 MSG). Carrying around unforgiveness is too heavy, and it gets in the way of your spiritual clothes. Is there anyone you need to forgive? Ask Jesus for help.

....

Thank You, Lord, for providing for me. Please show me how I can further Your kingdom by sharing what I have. I know that You are the very source of love, God. Help me get in the habit of "putting on" Your love every morning. It's the most important thing I can remember.

No Fear in Love

In this [union and fellowship with Him], love is completed and perfected with us, so that we may have confidence in the day of judgment [with assurance and boldness to face Him]; because as He is, so are we in this world. There is no fear in love [dread does not exist]. But perfect (complete, full-grown) love drives out fear, because fear involves [the expectation of divine] punishment, so the one who is afraid [of God's judgment] is not perfected in love [has not grown into a sufficient understanding of God's love]. We love, because He first loved us.

1 JOHN 4:17–19 AMP

- God is not mad at you. He is not going to punish you. He sees you through the love and sacrifice of Jesus. So you can approach Him without fear! Thank Him for this amazing truth as you come into His presence today.

- A person who fears God's wrath doesn't understand who they are in Christ. You don't have to work harder or be a better Christian to earn God's love and approval. Nothing you could ever do or not do could make Him love you more than He does right now. A lot of your friends and maybe even your family have trouble believing this. Bring those friends and family members to mind and pray for each one of them to start believing what Jesus has done for them and how God sees them. Pray for them to know how dearly loved they are.

- When you begin to believe who you are in Christ, it changes everything. You start living differently. You realize how deeply loved you are and it sets you free. As Jesus pours His love and His Spirit into your life, it spills over into the lives of those around you. Ask God to continue pouring His love, His truth, His peace, His joy, and His freedom into your life so that the people around you will notice a difference and want that for their lives.

....

You loved me first, God. That's how I know what love is. You laid down Your life for me. There is no greater love than that. I pray for my friends and family who are struggling with this idea. Let my life be a living example of what Your love looks like.

Strong Roots

"But blessed are those who trust in the LORD and have made the LORD their hope and confidence. They are like trees planted along a riverbank, with roots that reach deep into the water. Such trees are not bothered by the heat or worried by long months of drought. Their leaves stay green, and they never stop producing fruit."

JEREMIAH 17:7–8 NLT

- A tree with deep roots won't get toppled when the storms come. It's strongly attached to the ground. It grows deep and is able to find the water it needs to stay hydrated during a dry spell. How are your roots? Are you firmly planted in God's Word? Is your faith firm and strong enough to withstand the storms of life? Pray for God to grow your faith roots. Ask Him to increase your faith and make it strong enough to get you through hard times.

- Make this prayer from Paul to the Ephesians your own: "I pray that from his glorious, unlimited resources he will empower you with inner strength through his Spirit. Then Christ will make his home in your hearts as you trust in him. Your roots will grow down into God's love and keep you strong" (Ephesians 3:16–17 NLT). Pray for God to empower you with inner strength through His Spirit. Thank Jesus for making His home in your heart. Pray for strong roots of love.

- Ask the Holy Spirit to help you memorize this verse and bring it to mind when you need it: "Let your roots grow down into him, and let your lives be built on him. Then your faith will grow strong in the truth you were taught, and you will overflow with thankfulness" (Colossians 2:7 NLT).

- If you want God's favor and blessing on your life, trust in Him. Put your hope in Him and find your confidence in Him alone. Pray and ask God to help you do this very thing.

....

Lord, I want Your blessing and favor on my life. I pray that You would grow my faith deep into the roots of Your love. I want to build my life on You and Your truth. Plant a deep thankfulness in my heart for all the ways You've blessed me and my family. I want to produce fruit that lasts and sweetens the lives of those around me.

The Better Choice

As Jesus and the disciples continued on their way to Jerusalem, they came to a certain village where a woman named Martha welcomed him into her home. Her sister, Mary, sat at the Lord's feet, listening to what he taught. But Martha was distracted by the big dinner she was preparing. She came to Jesus and said, "Lord, doesn't it seem unfair to you that my sister just sits here while I do all the work? Tell her to come and help me." But the Lord said to her, "My dear Martha, you are worried and upset over all these details! There is only one thing worth being concerned about. Mary has discovered it, and it will not be taken away from her."

LUKE 10:38–42 NLT

- You've probably heard this story about Mary and Martha before. Martha was cooking and serving Jesus and His followers. This was expected of women during this time period. Mary was sitting at His feet, wanting to hear everything He had to say. Which woman do you identify with more? Are you always doing what is expected of you and getting things done? Or do you take time to hear from Jesus? Pray about this. Ask Jesus to help you slow down so that you can learn to hear His voice.

- Martha did what was expected while Mary went against the cultural norms to be with Jesus. Her sister got mad at her and even whined about it to Jesus. Jesus replied in love but also told Martha the truth. Mary made the better choice. This was risky behavior in that time period. Mary's choice made her sister mad, and the other people there probably looked down on her too. It's hard to go against the norms and follow Jesus. Do you struggle with this? Ask Jesus for courage to follow Him even when everyone else says you're making the wrong choice.

- Martha was so focused on getting things done that she forgot the power of the One she was hosting! Jesus could have fed everyone Himself when He was finished teaching. Ask God to help you keep your focus on Him instead of your problems.

....

Peer pressure is hard, Lord. Please give me the courage to follow You and do what my heart is telling me even when other people disagree. I want to choose You even when it's not the popular choice.

Don't Give Up

What a person plants, he will harvest. The person who plants selfishness, ignoring the needs of others— ignoring God!—harvests a crop of weeds. All he'll have to show for his life is weeds! But the one who plants in response to God, letting God's Spirit do the growth work in him, harvests a crop of real life, eternal life. So let's not allow ourselves to get fatigued doing good. At the right time we will harvest a good crop if we don't give up, or quit.

GALATIANS 6:7–9 MSG

- Remember that what you plant you will harvest. It's the law of sowing and reaping again. If you plant selfishness, you get weeds. If you plant the Spirit of God in your heart, you get real, eternal life. Which do you choose? Ask God to weed out all the selfishness in your life. Ask Him to plant His Spirit firmly in your heart instead.

- If you allow God to keep weeding out all the selfishness in you, you grow good, healthy fruit. . .if you don't give up. Ask God to give you determination and endurance. Ask Him to bless you with strength to get through the weeding and pruning so that you can enjoy a fruitful life.

- Quitters give up because they've run out of their own strength. They have nothing left to give, so they give up in defeat. But for followers of Jesus, we depend on His strength. Remember that His power shines through in our weakness. Allow Him to be your strength. Invite Him to empower you with His Spirit.

- Jesus tells a story of a very persistent woman in Luke 18:1–8. She never gave up, and she was rewarded for her persistence. Prayerfully read these scriptures today. What does Jesus want you to know about this story? Ask Him for guidance. Keep coming back to Him every day in prayer.

....

Lord, just like the persistent woman, help me to always pray and never give up. Weeding is hard and dirty work. I pray that You would continue weeding out any selfishness in me. I want my heart to be full of the fruit of Your Spirit. Plant a strong desire in me to meet with You every day. Thank You that I don't have to depend on my own strength. I'd much rather count on Yours instead.

Peace Rules

*And let the peace that comes from Christ rule in your
hearts. For as members of one body you are called to
live in peace. And always be thankful. Let the message
about Christ, in all its richness, fill your lives.
Teach and counsel each other with all the wisdom he
gives. Sing psalms and hymns and spiritual songs to
God with thankful hearts. And whatever you do or say,
do it as a representative of the Lord Jesus,
giving thanks through him to God the Father.*

COLOSSIANS 3:15-17 NLT

- The Amplified translation says that the
  peace of Christ is "the inner calm of one who
  walks daily with Him" and letting it rule in
  our hearts means that His peace is to be the
  "controlling factor in your hearts [deciding
  and settling questions that arise]" (Colossians
  3:15). Pray and ask God to bless you with an
  inner calm as you walk with Him every day.
  Ask Him to focus your mind on Him daily so
  that He is the answer to all your questions.

- When you let peace rule in your heart, it
  means that you aren't a drama queen, vying
  for attention or stirring up chaos. When problems come, and they will, you center your
  heart on Jesus and His power over anything.
  Ask God to forgive you for the times that

you've freaked out without turning to Him. Ask Him to give you wisdom and peace as you go to Him with your problems.

- Getting in the daily habit of praying and taking all your problems, worries, and concerns to Jesus can help you avoid a lot of drama in your life! Drama might be entertaining on Netflix, but in real life it's messy and exhausting. Go to God in prayer and bring Him everything that is weighing down your heart.

- When you're dealing with unwanted drama and problems, turn on the praise music! Thank God for His hand in your life and His peace in your heart.

....

Lord, please fill my heart with Your peace and let it rule. Help me focus on You daily—to look at You and Your power instead of my problems. Help me avoid unnecessary drama and chaos. I want to be known as a peaceful person who walks daily with You.

Perfect Peace

"I have told you these things, so that in Me you may have [perfect] peace. In the world you have tribulation and distress and suffering, but be courageous [be confident, be undaunted, be filled with joy]; I have overcome the world." [My conquest is accomplished, My victory abiding.]

John 16:33 AMP

- The world that God created is a beautiful place, but it's a messed-up place too. We live in a fallen world, and things won't be perfect again until Jesus returns. Jesus promises us that this world will have trouble, because it's not heaven. We can't expect it to be. Talk to Jesus about this. Let go of your expectations of what this world should be. Embrace the reality and goodness of God's peace and presence in the midst of a dark world.

- John 14:27 (NIV) says: "Peace I leave with you; my peace I give you. I do not give to you as the world gives. Do not let your hearts be troubled and do not be afraid." This is a verse to write down and ask the Holy Spirit to help you remember! The world says that peace must be the absence of problems. But that's not what Jesus says. He says that perfect peace is His presence and power in the midst of problems. So, we never have to be afraid. Thank God for this truth. Ask for His help to believe it.

- You'll experience tribulation, distress, and suffering in this world. But the perfect peace of Jesus offers you courage, confidence, and joy because He has overcome the world by the cross and the resurrection. He is alive to help you navigate the struggles of this life. Talk to Jesus about the trials you are currently experiencing. Accept the peace that He offers.

- How can you practice being peaceful? Do you have a special place where you can get alone with God daily and talk to Him about your life? Pray and ask for God to help you come up with a special time and place to be with Him and receive His peace every day.

....

Jesus, I want the perfect peace that You offer. I give You my expectations of what I want this world to be, and I embrace the reality that You are here to help me through every day of my life on this planet.

Blameless

*For God in all his fullness was pleased to live in Christ,
and through him God reconciled everything to himself.
He made peace with everything in heaven and on
earth by means of Christ's blood on the cross.
This includes you who were once far away from God.
You were his enemies, separated from him by your evil
thoughts and actions. Yet now he has reconciled you
to himself through the death of Christ in his physical
body. As a result, he has brought you into his own
presence, and you are holy and blameless as
you stand before him without a single fault.*

Colossians 1:19–22 NLT

- God wants you to see yourself the way He
  does. Because of Jesus, He sees you as holy
  and blameless as you stand before Him. . .
  without a single fault! Can you believe it?
  Picture this in your head as you come to God
  in prayer. Thank Him for what He's done for
  you. Accept His love.

- God knows everything you've ever done and
  He loves you anyway. You don't have to hide
  anything from God. You don't have to get
  all cleaned up first before you come to Him.
  Jesus is like the friend who shows up at your
  house unexpectedly and offers to help you
  clean up a big mess. He helps you do the

cleaning, every step of the way. Thank God for His amazing grace. Ask Jesus to help you get where you need to be on your faith journey and to help you clean up anything that needs cleaning.

- One of the enemy's goals is to attack your identity in Christ so that you won't know who you are and the power you have because of Christ living in you. Stand against any lies. Repent of believing anything but what God says about you. Ask for the Holy Spirit to empower you to believe and walk in the truth.

....

Heavenly Father, it's so hard to imagine that I'm completely clean before You. That I'm holy and blameless! But Your Word tells me it's true, and I know that Jesus paid the price for all of that. Help me never take that for granted. My holiness cost Jesus His life. Help me live my life in a way that shows my gratitude. Help me walk in the truth of who You say I am.

The Divine Power

Grace and peace be yours in abundance through the knowledge of God and of Jesus our Lord. His divine power has given us everything we need for a godly life through our knowledge of him who called us by his own glory and goodness. Through these he has given us his very great and precious promises, so that through them you may participate in the divine nature, having escaped the corruption in the world caused by evil desires.

2 PETER 1:2–4 NIV

- It can be hard to keep the faith as we live in this mixed-up world. Some things seem so fake, and we're not sure what to believe: fake news, fake profiles, fake eyelashes. But we can trust that God is real and is active in our lives in every moment. What can you do to remind yourself of the reality of God right now? Affirm your faith in Christ and thank God for His divine power.

- Is your life marked by grace and peace? Ask God to reveal the ways that He has blessed you with His grace and peace. Do you feel like you are lacking in these areas? Take these thoughts and feelings to Jesus and ask Him to speak to you.

- God's Word tells us that He has given us everything we need to live a life that is honoring to Him. Did you catch that? He has given us everything! Everything that God wants you to have and know right now is currently available to you. You don't have to wait until you finish school or get home from camp. You have everything you need to be close to God right now. Think about that. Thank God for that amazing blessing. Spend some time being close to Jesus today.

....

Jesus, I'm so blessed by Your divine power. I can't thank You enough for giving me absolutely everything I need to be close to You in each moment. Because of Your divine power, I am free to love You and be loved by You. I'm free to be me. I'm free to live life the way You created me to. I don't have to have a Bible degree to know You. I don't have to pretend to be something I'm not. The grace and peace You offer me right now is all that I need.

Work That Matters

Whatever you do [whatever your task may be],
work from the soul [that is, put in your very best effort],
as [something done] for the Lord and not for men,
knowing [with all certainty] that it is from the Lord
[not from men] that you will receive the inheritance
which is your [greatest] reward. It is the Lord
Christ whom you [actually] serve.

COLOSSIANS 3:23–24 AMP

- Since most of us spend all our days working on something (schoolwork, after-school job, homework, sports, etc.), it's important to seek God in this area. Pray that He would give you wisdom as you do the jobs you must get done.

- Whatever you decide to do, work at it with all your heart. Cutting corners and being lazy will only backfire. No matter what you're working on, it can be an act of worship to God. Your boss or your teacher might seem like the ultimate responder in whatever you are working on, but the Bible tells us it's actually God. How would you work differently if you had to hand your paper straight to Jesus? What would your job be like if Jesus was the one signing your time card? Talk to God about this. Ask Him for help in seeing that Jesus is the One you are actually serving as you do your schoolwork or work at your job.

- God sees you as you clean your room and do your chores at home. He cares about everything you're doing. When you realize you're actually serving and worshipping God as you work, you become a joy to your parents too. Ask God to help you with your chores. Pray for Him to give you joy in serving and helping around the house. Turning worship music on while you work always helps too!

- Pray about your future and ask God to lead you into the best job or ministry that uses the gifts and skills He gave you. Remember, all work can be kingdom work if you have the right attitude.

. . . .

Lord, please help me work willingly at whatever I do, and help me remember that it is all about You and for You anyway! Remind me about the big picture when I'm working so that I can give my very best for You. Help me work hard at the tasks You've given me and do the ones I don't enjoy with a good attitude.

Praying the Psalms

*I bow before your holy Temple as I worship. I praise
your name for your unfailing love and faithfulness;
for your promises are backed by all the honor of
your name. As soon as I pray, you answer me;
you encourage me by giving me strength. . . .
The LORD will work out his plans for my life—
for your faithful love, O LORD, endures forever.
Don't abandon me, for you made me.*

PSALM 138:2–3, 8 NLT

- *"I bow before your holy Temple as I worship."*
  Have you ever gotten on your knees to pray?
  Historically, people used to kneel before
  kings when asking their requests. The Bible
  tells us that Jesus knelt to pray sometimes
  too. Of course you can pray anytime, from
  anyplace, in any position, but sometimes it's a
  good thing to humble yourself before God
  and present your requests. Give it a try.

- *"I praise your name for your unfailing love and
  faithfulness; for your promises are backed by
  all the honor of your name."* Thank and praise
  God for His faithfulness and love for you. He
  always keeps His promises.

- *"As soon as I pray, you answer me; you
  encourage me by giving me strength."* God

hears your prayers, and He always answers. He might not always give you the answer you want, but He will always encourage you and give you the strength you need to get through anything. As you pray, look for His encouraging support and strength. Ask Him to speak to your heart and fill you with His strength.

- *"The LORD will work out his plans for my life."* Memorize this promise. Thank Him for it. Bring your plans and ideas to God and ask Him to help you sort them all out. He will lead and guide you if you invite Him to be a part of it.

- *"For your faithful love, O LORD, endures forever. Don't abandon me, for you made me."* God will never stop loving you. In fact, nothing can separate you from His love (Romans 8:38–39), and He has promised never to abandon you (Deuteronomy 31:8). Ask God to reveal His presence to you more and more as you walk with Him.

. . . .

Thank You for Your unfailing love and faithfulness to me, Lord. You have never left my side. Help me see You throughout my day. Remind me of Your constant presence.

Beyond the Bubble

So if you're serious about living this new resurrection life with Christ, act like it. Pursue the things over which Christ presides. Don't shuffle along, eyes to the ground, absorbed with the things right in front of you. Look up, and be alert to what is going on around Christ—that's where the action is. See things from his perspective. Your old life is dead. Your new life, which is your real life—even though invisible to spectators—is with Christ in God. He is your life. When Christ (your real life, remember) shows up again on this earth, you'll show up, too—the real you, the glorious you.

Colossians 3:1-4 MSG

- As a teen girl, it's easy to get caught up in the world around you: friends, family, school, church, sports. Is there anything else? Sometimes it can be hard to see anything beyond our bubbles because we become so entrenched in our daily lives. But if you're serious about following Jesus, you need to keep your eyes up. Go to God and ask Him for help to look beyond the bubble. Ask Him to give you a bigger picture of your life. . .an eternal perspective.

- Ask God to give you ideas about seeing beyond what's right in front of you. Have you prayed about going on a mission trip? Ask

God if that's something He would like for you to do.

- What kingdom work does God have for you? Ask Him to show you how He wants you to share His love with others. You could volunteer in children's ministry. You could be a Christian camp counselor. You could lead a Bible study at school. Ask Him to open doors for you to be His light and love to others.

- In this new life, you need a lot of support. Ask God to bring you close Christian friends who are on the same life path as you. Pray for your current friends to have eyes to see beyond the bubble and to fall in love with Jesus and His ways. Pray for your family to see God's great plans for their lives too.

....

Lord, please forgive me for the times I get sucked into my own little world. Help me see beyond the bubble. Please bring friends who love You and follow Your ways to walk alongside me as I do Your kingdom work.

Precious and Beautiful

*Don't be concerned about the outward beauty of fancy
hairstyles, expensive jewelry, or beautiful clothes. You
should clothe yourselves instead with the beauty that
comes from within, the unfading beauty of a gentle
and quiet spirit, which is so precious to God.*

1 PETER 3:3–4 NLT

- Do you ever wish you were created a little
  differently? Maybe with straight hair or
  smoother skin? God wants you to know that
  you are beautiful just the way you are! Ask
  God for help to accept yourself and your
  body just the way He made you.

- Get in front of a mirror. Ask God to be with
  you and speak truth to you as you bless every
  part of your body. Start at your feet and work
  your way up. Thank God for feet that get you
  where you need to go. Thank Him for your
  legs that are strong. Thank Him for arms to
  hug your family and friends. Thank Him specifically for every part of your amazing body.
  Ask God to continue blessing your body with
  health and strength. Ask Him to help you take
  good care of the body He gave you.

- The Bible says that people look at outward
  appearances but God looks at the heart

(1 Samuel 16:7). A truly beautiful person shines from the inside out. Ask God to give you a pure heart that will light up the rest of your body. Pray for your friends that need to know how beautiful they really are.

- You don't need the best hair or designer clothes to be precious to God. You are His princess, and He created you just the way you are. Thank Him for your smile. Thank Him for making you with the special traits that only you have.

- Did you know that your body is known as a temple of the Holy Spirit (1 Corinthians 6:19–20)? So God wants you to honor Him with your body. Talk to God about this. Ask Him to help you honor Him with your body.

....

God, please create in me a beautiful and pure heart. I want to follow You, and I want my beauty to shine from inside. Thanks for creating me just the way I am. Help me see myself as You see me. Please give me wisdom to know how to take care of my body well.

Virtue and Self-Control

*For this very reason, make every effort to add to
your faith goodness; and to goodness, knowledge;
and to knowledge, self-control; and to self-control,
perseverance; and to perseverance, godliness;
and to godliness, mutual affection;
and to mutual affection, love.*

2 PETER 1:5–7 NIV

- We don't hear a lot about virtue and self-control
  in today's culture. Being a girl of virtue means
  that you pursue goodness and purity instead of
  trying to fit in with the crowd. Pray about this.
  Ask God to help you be bold and courageous,
  to help you stand up for what's right and have
  self-control in tempting situations.

- Our enemy, Satan, is out to trip up young
  people in any way he can. He often aims his
  arrows right at your purity—telling you that
  you're not cool if you don't wear what other
  girls are wearing, trying to get you to believe
  you're not beautiful unless you have a boy-
  friend, urging you to look at something online
  that you know you shouldn't, etc. Those are
  all tricks and lies from the pit of hell. Don't
  believe them! Instead, ask God to fill you up
  with His power to overcome all the tricks of
  the enemy.

- Bring to mind any of your friends that are stuck in the trap of fitting in. Ask God to let them see what they mean to Him. Pray that they'll come to know the truth of how God sees them. Pray for your believing friends too. That they will be strong and avoid temptation. That they will seek God's will for their lives.

- Lamentations 3:22–23 (ESV) says: "The steadfast love of the LORD never ceases; his mercies never come to an end; they are new every morning; great is your faithfulness." If you feel like you've made a bunch of mistakes today, talk to God about them. Ask Him to forgive you, to restore your relationship with Him, and to purify your heart. Our great God forgives you and loves you. Pray for any of your friends who need a fresh start.

....

Lord, I want to be a girl of virtue. A classy girl who is known to love and honor You. Help me not to cave to peer pressure but to be a good example. Please give me courage to stand up for what's right. I pray for my friends who struggle with this. Help me encourage them.

Living for the One True God

We know that God's children do not make a practice of sinning, for God's Son holds them securely, and the evil one cannot touch them. We know that we are children of God and that the world around us is under the control of the evil one. And we know that the Son of God has come, and he has given us understanding so that we can know the true God. And now we live in fellowship with the true God because we live in fellowship with his Son, Jesus Christ. He is the only true God, and he is eternal life. Dear children, keep away from anything that might take God's place in your hearts.

1 JOHN 5:18–21 NLT

- As a child of God, you are held secure in the arms of Jesus. The enemy can't defeat you because of who you are in Christ. Can you picture this as you pray? Ask Jesus to let you see Him holding you safe.

- Our God is the only true God. Those are fighting words in our culture. But it doesn't make them any less true. Think about this quote by pastor Timothy Keller: "The founders of every major religion said, 'I'll show you how to find God.' Jesus said, 'I am God who has come to find you.' " Go to Jesus in prayer and thank Him for coming to find you and for making a way to be with Him for eternity. Ask Jesus to help you show His love to others so that they can know His abundant and eternal life too.

- Ask for God's help to steer clear of anything that could take His place in your heart. It's been said that the enemy doesn't show up wearing horns so that you can easily recognize him as evil. No, he shows up looking like everything you ever wanted. Ask God to help you see through the enemy's schemes to trick you and lead you away. Prayerfully put your armor on today.

. . . .

Jesus, thank You for coming for me. The only way I know how to love is because You loved me first (1 John 4:19). My faith is based on Your transformational love alone. Help me share that truth with others. Let them know I'm one of Your kids because I love well. I want to stay close to You, Jesus.

God's Favor and Blessing

"The eyes of the LORD watch over those who do right, and his ears are open to their prayers. But the LORD turns his face against those who do evil."

1 PETER 3:12 NLT

- When you are living for Jesus, God's eyes lovingly watch over you, and His ears are open to hear your prayers. Do you want that closeness and protection from God? Talk to Him about this. Let Him know your heart. Ask for wisdom and help to live for Jesus. Ask Him to show you what living for Jesus looks like.

- What would it feel like to have God turn His face from you? If you are continuing to sin on purpose, 1 Peter tells us that's what happens. Would you rather have God for you or against you? Is there anything you need to confess to God? A sin that you keep on doing on purpose even though you know it's wrong? Ask God to forgive you and help you change. Ask for His blessing on your life again.

- Many times we blame God when bad things happen to us. But if we are making bad choices repeatedly, natural consequences happen. It's that law of sowing and reaping again. That's just the way things work. Are you blaming God for the natural consequences you're receiving for your own choice? Confess this to God. Ask Him to show you the truth.

- Commit your heart to Jesus again. Ask for His blessing on your life as you make steps to live for Him. Ask Him to continue pointing toward His will and His ways in your life and that He would give you the strength and the wisdom to follow through.

- Pray for any of your friends or family members who are choosing to live apart from God and His blessing. Ask for God to get ahold of their hearts. Pray that they will repent and turn to God. Pray for His will in their lives.

....

Lord, I want Your favor and blessing on my life. I want to know that we're walking this path together. Please speak to me and continue leading me in Your truth. I commit my whole heart to You, Jesus. I want to follow Your ways because I love You and I trust that You know what's best for me.

My True Inheritance

*LORD, you alone are my inheritance, my cup of blessing.
You guard all that is mine. The land you have given me
is a pleasant land. What a wonderful inheritance! I will
bless the LORD who guides me; even at night my heart
instructs me. I know the LORD is always with me. I will
not be shaken, for he is right beside me. No wonder my
heart is glad, and I rejoice. My body rests in safety.*

PSALM 16:5–9 NLT

- The psalmist reminds us that Christ alone is our inheritance. Give thanks to God in prayer that He promises us restored bodies in a new heaven and a new earth where there will be no tears and no pain (Revelation 21:4), and that we will reign with Jesus forever (Revelation 22:1–5).

- It's important to remember that while you might work hard to earn money for "things," you can't take anything with you when you leave this world. Job 1:21 (AMP) says: "Naked (without possessions) I came [into this world] from my mother's womb, and naked I will return there. The LORD gave and the LORD has taken away; blessed be the name of the LORD." Is there anything you need to gain an eternal perspective on? Any "thing" you might be holding on to a little too tightly? Ask Jesus to help you view things in proper perspective, as gifts to hold on to loosely and with thanksgiving.

- With an eternal perspective, you can see problems and heartache in their proper light. Weeping may last for a little while, but joy will come (Psalm 30:5). So you don't have to be shaken when you get bad news. Jesus is with you always. Bring any sadness or heartache to Jesus. Picture yourself carrying it all to Him. He wants to help carry your load. Ask Him to help you see things through His eyes.

....

Lord, I know You have eternal joy planned for those of us who believe. I believe the truth that You will wipe away every tear and there will be no more death. Thank You for this amazing promise. Help me live like I believe it. Help me lift my eyes to see things from Your perspective. Show me anything that I'm holding on to too tightly. Thank You for carrying my load.

Nothing Is Outside of His Control

We look at this Son and see the God who cannot be seen. We look at this Son and see God's original purpose in everything created. For everything, absolutely everything, above and below, visible and invisible, rank after rank after rank of angels— everything got started in him and finds its purpose in him. He was there before any of it came into existence and holds it all together right up to this moment.

COLOSSIANS 1:15-17 MSG

- Does something in your life feel too big—or too little—for God? Is there a problem or an issue that you are holding on to and trying to figure out all by yourself? Bring that to Jesus in prayer. Ask Him to show you what you are holding on to.

- It's time to confess the truth. Conviction happens when God pricks our hearts about something that does not line up with His will for us. The amazing thing is that God's conviction is clean. He doesn't want you wallowing in shame and self-pity. Romans 2:4 tells us that it's God's loving-kindness that brings us to repentance. His love is what draws out the darkness and brings it to light. Ask God to shine His light on any sin in your life. Ask forgiveness for any area or problem that you've believed to be too big for God to handle.

- God is over all and in all and through all. He holds all things together. . ."right up to this moment." He knows everything and is certainly aware of everything that concerns you. What is concerning you in this moment? Bring your thoughts and feelings to Jesus. Invite Him to show you the truth.

- What does Jesus want to help you with that has felt outside of His care? No problem, big or small, is too much. It is hard to believe that the God of all creation knows and cares about you, but the Bible tells us it is true. Sit with God in thankfulness and praise.

....

I'm so amazed, Lord, that You truly care so much for me. I bring all my problems and worries to You right now. I trust that You want to help me through every little thing. And every big thing too. Shine Your healing light on any area of my life that needs You in it. I trust in Your unfailing love for me.

Praying the Names of Jesus

For to us a child is born, to us a son is given, and the government will be on his shoulders. And he will be called Wonderful Counselor, Mighty God, Everlasting Father, Prince of Peace.

<small>Isaiah 9:6 niv</small>

- The names of Jesus help us know what kind of God we serve. His name is powerful, and He offers everything your heart needs. Isaiah tells us first that He is called Wonderful Counselor. Jesus holds all the wisdom and knowledge we could ever need (Colossians 2:3). He has the perfect answer for every one of your questions. Thank Him for His wonderful knowledge. Ask Him to give you wisdom as you seek Him every day.

- Jesus is our Mighty God. He is a warrior, able to fight all our battles (Exodus 14:14; Exodus 15:3; Deuteronomy 20:4; 2 Chronicles 20:17). In what situation do you need God to fight for you? Where do you need Him to shield and protect you? Talk to Him about this.

- Jesus is our Everlasting Father. As Jesus welcomed the little children in His lap (Matthew 19:14), so He welcomes you. Can you picture yourself climbing onto the lap of Jesus and letting Him love you like a good and perfect father? Maybe you have a great relationship with your earthly father, or a not-so-good one. Allow Jesus to meet the "father" needs in your heart. He can fill the empty spaces that no earthly father ever could.

- Jesus is our Prince of Peace. Romans 5:1–2 (NIV) says: "Therefore, since we have been justified through faith, we have peace with God through our Lord Jesus Christ, through whom we have gained access by faith into this grace in which we now stand." Jesus made it possible for us to have peace with God. Praise God for making a way for us to stand before Him in peace. Ask Him to bring your family and friends into relationship with Him as well.

Your names mean so much to me, Jesus. I praise You for being my Wonderful Counselor, my Mighty God, my Everlasting Father, and my Prince of Peace. You are so good to me, and You've made a way to take care of every need I have.

Why Jesus Came

*The Spirit of the Sovereign LORD is upon me, for the
LORD has anointed me to bring good news to the poor.
He has sent me to comfort the brokenhearted and to
proclaim that captives will be released and prisoners
will be freed. He has sent me to tell those who mourn
that the time of the LORD's favor has come, and with
it, the day of God's anger against their enemies.
To all who mourn in Israel, he will give a crown
of beauty for ashes, a joyous blessing instead of
mourning, festive praise instead of despair. In their
righteousness, they will be like great oaks that
the LORD has planted for his own glory.*

ISAIAH 61:1–3 NLT

- Jesus came for you in so many ways. We're
  going to talk to Him about several of these as
  we pray today. God's Word tells us that Jesus
  came to comfort those with broken hearts.
  Are you hurting about something today?
  Bring it before Jesus. Do you have a friend or
  family member with a broken heart? Pray for
  them to find comfort in Christ alone.

- Jesus came to offer freedom. When God
  frees your heart from the prison of darkness,
  you can live life "freely and lightly" (Matthew
  11:30 MSG). Do you feel imprisoned by anything right now? Maybe a group of friends,

an addiction, or a lie you are believing? Ask Jesus to break your chains and free you. He loves doing that!

- Jesus came to bring joy and blessing instead of mourning and despair. Are you in need of more joy and blessing in your life? Turn in your sadness and depression. Bring it to Jesus. Let Him carry your heavy load. Ask for an exchange.

- Jesus came to give crowns of beauty from ashes. Have you ever had anything explode into flames in your life? Do you need Jesus to bring beauty to something that seems hopeless and dead? Ask Him. You are the beloved daughter of the King.

....

You came to set me free, Jesus, and I'm so thankful! Thank You for giving me hope and bringing healing and wholeness to my heart. Thank You for showing me that I'm Your beloved daughter and that You care about the things I care about. Help me have courage to face the hard things in life, knowing that You're always with me.

People Problems

You keep track of all my sorrows. You have collected all my tears in your bottle. You have recorded each one in your book. My enemies will retreat when I call to you for help. This I know: God is on my side! I praise God for what he has promised; yes, I praise the LORD for what he has promised. I trust in God, so why should I be afraid? What can mere mortals do to me?

PSALM 56:8–11 NLT

- Does God care about the things that make you sad? Yes. The Bible says He counts your tears and writes them down. One of Jesus' nicknames was "Man of Sorrows" because He was rejected by people (even some of His own friends) and He was very familiar with pain and suffering. Whatever you're going through, Jesus understands because He's been there. Talk to Him about it. Have you ever felt left out or not good enough for other people? Ask Jesus what He wants you to know about that. Your tears matter to God.

- Remember that the name of Jesus is so powerful (Philippians 2:10), and when you speak His name and call on Him for help, the enemy has to leave. Is there some fear you're dealing with? Call on the name of Jesus for help.

- When you trust God, you don't have to worry about other people. You might have heard the saying that we all put our pants on one leg at a time. That means that everyone is human. The Bible says that God is no respecter of persons, meaning He doesn't show favoritism (Acts 10:34; Romans 2:11). The president of the United States has no more pull with God than a janitor. He sees us all just as we are: human. Ask God for help and confidence around other people. There is no need to be afraid just because someone seems more important than you. You are God's daughter—royalty! Ask God for His help to be yourself around all people.

....

Lord, You know that so many of my tears have come from being hurt by other people. This makes me scared to be myself sometimes. Help me see myself as You see me! I'm Your child, and that makes me royalty. Help me see others as they are too: human beings who need You. Help me be exactly who You created me to be.

Final Truths

"Don't be afraid, I've redeemed you. I've called your name. You're mine. When you're in over your head, I'll be there with you. When you're in rough waters, you will not go down. When you're between a rock and a hard place, it won't be a dead end—because I am God, your personal God, the Holy of Israel, your Savior. I paid a huge price for you: all of Egypt, with rich Cush and Seba thrown in! That's how much you mean to me! That's how much I love you! I'd sell off the whole world to get you back, trade the creation just for you."

Isaiah 43:1–4 MSG

- Picture Jesus saying these words from Isaiah to you as you pray. How do they make you feel? Do you believe that God loves you this much? When God Himself tells you who you are, it changes everything. Let Him speak to your heart. You are His beloved daughter. He would trade the whole world to get you back. Ask Him to help you believe these truths and live your life like you believe them.

- If you're going through a rough time and feel like you're stuck with no options, God says it won't be a dead end. Because He is with you—your own personal God—there will always be another way out. You have direct access to the One who sees and knows all.

Hard times are never what they seem. Are you feeling stuck? Ask God to provide a way out. Listen for His leading.

- Focus on these final truths: You are God's girl. His princess. His royal daughter. He calls you by name. He knows you and loves you more than you could ever imagine. You are chosen. You are free. You are a new creation. A temple of the Holy Spirit. You are light in this world. God sees you as perfect because of Jesus. He wants to walk with you and talk to you moment by moment. Pray about these truths. Ask God to plant them firmly in your heart.

....

Your words of love fill my heart with joy and hope, Lord. Thank You for showing me who I really am. Because of Jesus, I come boldly into Your presence and You receive me with love. Continue speaking to me, Lord. Help me know Your voice and follow You all the days of my life.

Topical index

Scripture Index